"In these devotions the author takes the reader on a riveting quest by sharing helpful experiences and information. This is significant for every person who aspires to serve our precious Lord as a nurse. Such a calling is so much more than just being a nurse, and makes nursing a noble calling that has eternal ramifications. These devotionals are a must read for every nurse to have, to treasure, and for reference when this important calling momentarily becomes burdensome."

REV. DR. JOHN HIBMA
Doctorate, Fuller Theological Seminary, Los Angeles
Reformed Pastor, Five Churches in California and Michigan
Chaplain, The Michigan Home for Veterans
School Teacher

"Kathy Seif gives practical advice and scripture readings for young and experienced nurses alike. This is done with a deep sense of faith, which in the dark times of individuals, organizations, and nations is our only light. Anyone who doubts the need for spirituality in healthcare has either not practiced long or has not listened to the need of their patients."

DR. PAUL O. FARR M.D.
Past Chief of Staff, Saint Mary's Mercy Medical Center
Chairman, Saint Mary's Mercy Medical Center's Board of Trustees
Gastroenterologist, actively practicing in the Grand Rapids, Michigan area

"Kathy has written a series of weekly devotionals specifically geared to nurses and student nurses. Her writing demonstrates her personal knowledge of her profession's frustrations and joys. More importantly, she shares her reformed faith by putting her faith into action in her world. In addition to the nurses for whom this was intended, I think this devotional would be very helpful for a broader group of healthcare providers."

GRACE OLDENBROEK-SHEARER, MBA
Former Senior Vice President of Operations, Saint Mary's Mercy Medical Center
Chief Executive Officer, West Michigan Heart

"Devoted Christian wife, mother, grandmother and nurse, Kathy Seif, reveals her own caring heart in these devotions. She invites the reader to delve deep in the Bible to find strength to endure the long hours of difficult situations, faith to step forward into the unknown of a professional career, and courage to bring hope to hurting people. Many nursing students will be able to relate to Kathy's personal faith journey. She offers healing with her words."

REV EVAN HEEREMA
Former Pastor of Congregational Life, Christian Reformed Churches in Washington
and Michigan
Volunteer Hospital Chaplain, Spectrum Health—Butterworth Campus
Professor, Reformed Bible College

THE CALLING

A Weekly Devotional for Student Nurses and Seasoned Nurses

Written By Kathy A. Seif R.N.

Belleville, Ontario, Canada

THE CALLING
A Weekly Devotional for Student Nurses and Seasoned Nurses
Copyright © 2002, Kathy Seif

All Scripture quotations are from *The Holy Bible, New International Version*. Copyright © 1973, 1978, 1984 International Bible Society. Used by permission of Zondervan Publishing House. All rights reserved.

"They'll Know We Are Christians" by Peter Scholtes. "Jesus is All the World to Me" by Will Thompson. ©1966 F.E.L. Assigned 1991 to Lorenz Publishing Company. All rights reserved. Used with permission.

National Library of Canada Cataloguing in Publication

Seif, Kathy A. (Kathy Ann), 1947-
The calling : a weekly devotional for student nurses and seasoned nurses / Kathy A. Seif.

Includes bibliographical references.
ISBN 1-55306-449-6

1. Nurses—Prayer-books and devotions—English. I. Title.

BV4596.N8S42 2002   242'.68   C2002-905436-2

For more information or to order additional copies, please contact:

Kathy's Care Connection
c/o Kathy Seif
6925 Edgeview SW
Byron Center, MI 49315

Guardian Books is an imprint of *Essence Publishing,* a Christian Book Publisher dedicated to furthering the work of Christ through the written word. For more information, contact:

44 Moira Street West, Belleville, Ontario, Canada K8P 1S3.
Phone: 1-800-238-6376 • Fax: (613) 962-3055.
E-mail: info@essencegroup.com • Internet: www.essencegroup.com

To my perpetually encouraging husband, Andrew Derk,
and my poetry-composing daughter, Tami Seif-Pothoven,
who shares my love of nursing.

Contents

Purpose

I seek to stave off the future progression of the mounting problem of a shortage of nurses. Not only is the number of students entering the profession dwindling, but the numbers of newly trained nurses suffering premature burn out has also risen drastically. We nurses care for others exceptionally well, however, we fail to adequately nurture our own bodies and souls. I desire every nurse to become aware of what a noble calling he or she has. I propose to give encouragement through Scripture which will give you strength to not only endure for the long haul, but to truly feel satisfaction in the daily workout of nursing as your profession of choice.

Your Personal Care Plan

You have embarked upon or have been embroiled in a profession which I consider a calling, hence the title of this book of devotions for nurses. I personally believe that no other profession can ever be more gratifying, demanding, intellectually stimulating, and diversified as nursing. The level of service you provide to your patients will multiply exponentially the rewards you receive professionally and personally.

No other profession demands the same variety of skills or hours of service. Never will you stagnate intellectually because medical technology, pharmacology, computerized charting, etc. change so frequently. Then there is the diversity of nursing! You have an unprecedented choice of modalities: hospital nursing, home care, occupational nursing, extended care facility work, school nursing, rehabilitation nursing, mental health care, parish nursing, and doctor's office nursing. Additionally, you have the subsets of specialties like pediatrics, obstetrics, oncology, orthopedics, emergency, or surgical nursing to name a few.

So, with all these opportunities available, why would I consider nursing a calling? If nursing was a high-profile occupation with elevated financial benefits and premium work hours, it would be in high demand as a profession, without the need for inner urgings. In reality, nursing is by no means any of the above. Much of your work is demeaning and gross. The remunerations are miniscule when compared to other professions requiring equal amounts of education. The shifts and days of work are extremely inconvenient.

For these reasons, I felt the need to give encouragement and re-energization to our profession by supporting the caregiver. This is what I propose to do with these devotionals.

Reunion Time

Do not forsake your friend and the friend of your father, and do not go to your brother's house when disaster strikes you—better a neighbor nearby than a brother far away (Prov. 27:10).

It's a sunny and warm fall day. You and your mother and/or father have been working feverishly since the alarm went off this morning. The mini-van has been packed to the brim with your belongings and is now weaving its' way through a maze of cars, vans, and trucks lined helter-skelter in the road in front of your college dorm.

A college freshie! What a feeling! How confident you felt as a high school senior less than three months ago. Where has it all gone now? Everything is new and big and scary. Everyone else looks calm, busy, and self-assured.

Your parents chatter positive comments in your ear while you all carry things into the room your Residence Director pointed you to. The room is bare and cold. None of the familiar feelings of your room at home are here. As you pile your boxes of clothes on the floor by the bunk beds, you smile and act excited about your mother's observations, but your heart is palpitating.

The hubbub is broken by a familiar voice shouting, "Hey, Betsy! We've got the same dorm." There stands one of your acquaintances from South High. Now your smile broadens to it's fullest, relief floods your soul, and you run to embrace Karen.

"Where is your room?" you ask.

"I'm at the end of the hall, one floor up? Boy, am I glad to see your friendly face! I'm scared to death, aren't you?"

"Yeah, but now we can do this together. Quickly show me your room, and I'll come to see you when we're all done unloading the van."

Prayer

Thank you Lord Jesus for planning my first day the way you have. I'm so grateful you loved me enough to think of me even though I was obviously "too busy" to take time for you this morning. I promise to try harder tomorrow to consult you at the start of my day. Please bless my new friend for reaching out to me at just the right time. In your compassionate and always faithful name I pray, Amen

Potluck

Let the morning bring me word of your unfailing love, for I have put my trust in you.
Show me the way I should go for to you I lift up my soul (Ps. 143:8).

"We advise you to give much thought to your choice of roommates for next fall," you remembered the dean of women saying at college orientation day last spring. "Some of the best friends become worst enemies after living together for nine months. You might want to have the computer pick your roommate to avoid losing a friend." That sounded like a wise thing to do, and several college students you talked to at yearbook-signing night had agreed with this idea. You made a judgment call and went "potluck."

It sounded logical at the time, but now you wonder. What if the computer misinterpreted your comments on the admissions form and you get stuck with a real weirdo? You're worried she might be an atheist, short-tempered, and sloppy; or worse yet—gorgeous, a super athlete, and a brain. You just know that she'll be hard to live with for nine months, or you'll feel totally inferior all year because she has "everything."

Read verses 7 and 8 again of our scripture for this week. Each time you feel tempted to worry, remember to trust in your God. He knows the way (and circumstances) you are going to be living in today, tomorrow, and the next day. He loves you and will give you just the right roommate to cause your spiritual growth. Walk with God and maybe, just maybe, you are about to meet your best friend for life!

Prayer

Help me, Lord I pray, to be a faithful friend to my new roommate. I know you have chosen her for me. Please help me to love her as you have loved me, in spite of my faults. In your son, Jesus', name, who loved me before I even knew Him, Amen.

Signs

Since you are my rock and my fortress, for the sake of your name lead and guide me (Ps. 31:3).

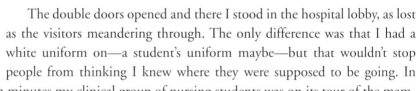

The double doors opened and there I stood in the hospital lobby, as lost as the visitors meandering through. The only difference was that I had a white uniform on—a student's uniform maybe—but that wouldn't stop people from thinking I knew where they were supposed to be going. In about fifteen minutes my clinical group of nursing students was on its tour of the mammoth building. I still swear to this day they have rooms the sole purpose of which is to help people get lost, because they can't possibly all have a vital use. Our instructor was saying, "First floor contains x-ray, ultrasound, CT Scan, M.R.I. scan, etc. Second floor is for outpatient services, shortstay patients, and pre-admission testing. Surgery is on the third floor along with the recovery room. Endoscopy occupies the fourth floor." The tour continued in this manner until every unit had been traversed.

At the end of the tour both, Karen and I agreed that we were only slightly more informed than when we started. At least we remembered where the café and the public restrooms were placed and, ah yes, the three banks of elevators, even if we weren't quite sure which led to which unit. Though my knowledge was woefully small, being able to find these three places did prove to be very helpful.

Likewise, in your spiritual journey there are three people who will prove to be very valuable. These are God the Father, Jesus Christ His Son, and the Holy Spirit. Whenever you feel overwhelmed with life as Karen and I did on the tour of this immense hospital building, these helpers can make all the difference in how secure you feel. God the Father is always willing and anxious to lead you in the proper direction. Jesus Christ is our example of what to say and what to do in every life situation. The Holy Spirit is our dynamics and dramatics coach. He understands exactly what we are feeling and knows the language of our tears and joys to translate in petition to our Father in heaven. They are waiting patiently. Are you humble enough to ask for their assistance? It's awfully hard to navigate the maze of life on our own. Wouldn't you like some free help?

Prayer

Dear Father, please be my lead man today. Jesus, I'm just learning how to be a nurse. There is so much that I don't know. I will follow your example; will you give me the proper words to say and the compassion I need to be your servant in this profession? Holy Spirit, I ask you to help me set a spiritual tone in all my behavior. I admit that I can't do this without your help. Forgive me when I strut out on my own, because I know myself and am aware that, many times, I will try to be too independent. Please lead and guide me along my way. In Jesus' name, Amen.

Farewells

A man of many companions may come to ruin, but there is a friend who sticks closer than a brother (Prov. 18:24).

Take a few moments to remember your high school graduation day, just a few months, or possibly a few years ago. Do you recollect the feelings you experienced during practice and the actual ceremony? Or, the next morning as you stood in the school parking lot after your class all-nighter? The desperate need to talk some more or give one last hug to the special friends whose relationship to you will never quite be the same again after you say "good-bye" today?

Your friends and acquaintances are meeting with you for pizza tonight before they split in four directions, headed for their various colleges and vocational schools. There's that old feeling surfacing again! Will you be friends yet when you get together at Christmas break? Will future jobs tear you all apart to different corners of the country? Proverbs 18:24 states: "*there is a friend that sticks closer than a brother,*" That passage refers, of course, to Jesus Christ. Because of His omnipresence, He is always with you and your friends. He will never desert you if you hurt His feelings. He is in control of all your circumstances, so all your relationships have already been planned. Rest in faith on His wisdom to hold the friendships you truly depend on securely into eternity. Remember, if you are a Christian, you will never have to say "good-bye" to your best friend, Jesus.

Prayer

My dear Friend and Savior, thank you, once again, for these wonderful friendships. Whenever I feel the pangs of loneliness, remind me that you stick closer than a brother. Ensure my love for these special people, and theirs for me, into the foreseeable future and eternity. Please keep us close to each other, and to you, no matter how much time or how many miles may separate us. In Jesus' name, Amen.

Cast Out

Though my father and mother forsake me, the LORD will receive me (Ps. 27:10).

You've just discovered you're an orphan! The minute you moved to college, little sister moved into your room at home. It feels like you've been cast out with the trash. When you do go home—as if you ever care to go there again now—there is no place to call your own. It feels like your family couldn't wait for you to leave, and you are no longer a part of their lives. They don't even miss you!

Julian Jaynes' analogy of a ferris wheel seems to fit your situation perfectly:

"There is an awkward moment at the top of a ferris wheel when, having come up the inside curvature, where we are facing into a firm structure of confident girders, suddenly that structure disappears, and we are thrust out into the sky for the outward curve down. Such perhaps is the present moment."[1]

That feeling of total security inside the "girders" of a loving family has just been replaced with the sinking feeling of fear. The anxiety builds as you are plunged over the edge of the "curve" into life totally on your own and supposedly without support.

Read again our psalm of the week. You are never alone. Your God is always with you and will never forsake you! You can face the world without the back-up you're so accustomed to having. The Lord will guide you and surround you.

Maybe in the future you will discover, as I did, that you really are not a castaway. Sure your sister is in your room, but she just called to explain that she has neatly boxed up all "your" possessions so they won't get broken, and she plans on moving out and into her old room whenever you come home. She had ended by saying she hopes you come home very often. She misses you, and said, "Thank you for letting me use your room for a while."

Prayer

Dear Father in heaven, thank you from the depths of my heart for always being with me in the panicky times of life. And please give a blessing to my family for being so loving and supportive. In Jesus' name, Amen

Faith Moves the Decimal Points

"Do not set your heart on what you will eat or drink; do not worry about it.... your Father knows that you need them. But seek his kingdom, and these things will be given to you as well" (Luke 12:29-31).

Med-Surg. book – $63.95
O.B. text – $53.95
Peds. – $99.65
Nutrition – $32.50
Dictionary – $35.00
Psych. – $27.95
Pharmacology – $54.50
Tuition – $13,690
Etc.

No problem. If I sell most of my clothes, work thirty hours a week in addition to my classes, don't eat anything but Spaghetti O's and macaroni and cheese, and collect pop cans for the ten-cent deposit, I should be able to pay for them before the end of the term. To describe nursing school as expensive is quickly becoming an understatement. With rising costs, it is all too easy to be overwhelmed by the menagerie of ways to increase debt, and the miniscule avenues to make the necessary monthly payments.

God has, however, promised to take care of us in all of life's challenges. We don't have to worry. If worrying won't add a day to our lives, as it says in our Matthew passage for this week's reading, it's doubtful it will move the decimal point over on our loan statement. Fortunately, the Bible says that faith can move mountains. So pray to your Father for all your needs, and have faith that He hears you and will grant your requests. Petition the Lord and see if that decimal point doesn't edge over just a bit until it is gradually manageable month by month.

Prayer

Lord, I'm drowning in debt, and I'm afraid. I need your help to stop worrying and to start trusting you. Show me where to go, what to do, how to balance all the demands on my time and meager resources. Make me willing to do my part as I lean on you for support and direction. In Jesus' name, Amen.

Molding a Nurse

Yet, O LORD, you are our Father. We are the clay, you are the potter; we are all the work of your hand (Isa. 64:8).

I was so excited the day the order blanks came for my nursing equipment! Once the orders came in I knew I would really feel like a nurse. I was quite sick of having only Anatomy & Physiology textbooks to indicate what profession I was pursuing. So, I eagerly ordered a stethoscope, careful to pick out the perfect color, pretty, but one that wouldn't show the dirt, a blood pressure cuff, penlight, and bandage scissors. Then, in a few weeks, the orders had been filled. I sat on my bed with my box of "toys" in front of me. I looked at my equipment with excitement, then with fear. It occurred to me that I could hang that stethoscope around my neck or put it against someone's chest, but I didn't know what I was listening for. I could probably place the cuff on a patient's arm correctly, but I didn't yet know how to take a blood pressure. In fact, the only comforting piece of equipment I had purchased was the bandage scissors. After all, I had learned to cut in kindergarten.

27

Studying my textbooks, listening to my instructors' admonitions, and putting it all together with common sense and hospital protocol would gradually mold me into a nurse. Now, the next step I would need to take, and would encourage you to take, would be to not just become a nurse, but a Christian nurse. God can take your nursing skills and mold them into a service for others and as an offering to His glory. How? By your study of His textbook, the Bible; by following the Holy Spirit's guidance; and by becoming more Christ-like in your compassion for your patients. Then you will become not just an R.N., B.S.N., you will be molded into a Christian nurse who is diligent in all her work, loving to all personalities, and giving praise to God the Father by her attitude and level of integrity.

Prayer

Mold me and make me according to your will, O Lord. I want to become not just an R.N. I want to be a Christian R.N. Please give me the intelligence I need to learn and retain the vast amount of information I will need to utilize to make strong nursing judgments. I also request wisdom with setting priorities on the job, and in my personal life. In Jesus' name I pray, Amen.

Fantastic Fortification

Praise our God, O peoples, let the sound of his praise be heard; he has preserved our lives and kept our feet from slipping (Ps. 66:8-9).

"We never really become truly spiritual by sitting down and wishing to become so. You must undertake something so great that you cannot accomplish it unaided."[2]

When I have lost control and am desperate, I inevitably call out to God. Even those who have never been Christians find peace in prayer to God in times of severe stress, such as wartime or natural disasters. I'm sure you have had many times during your high school days and nurses' training so far, when you knew only God could give you the strength to succeed or simply survive.

This week, let's each worship and praise our tremendously powerful God. Feel His love and the depth of His concern for you. Consider His power—its force. Remember His creativity—its beauty. Be aware of His presence—its peace. Notice His generosity— its abundance. Now recall what He has done for you, raise a prayer of thanksgiving to Him, and praise Him with your mouth and thoughts this week.

29

Prayer

Jesus, my Savior, I can never thank you enough for the salvation you made possible for me. Because you orchestrated my adoption as God's child, every day I will celebrate your goodness. I praise you for the beauty of the human body you have woven together. Each day, as I study Anatomy and Physiology, I am learning more about just how intricate you made it. I confess that I need your power each day to retain all I need to know to serve my patients properly. Thank you for giving me peace in my decision of occupations to pursue, Amen

Robed in White

"Come now, let us reason together," says the LORD. *"Though your sins are like scarlet, they shall be as white as snow…"* (Isa. 1:18).

What is your perception of white: purity, perfection, professionalism? Your uniformed image in the mirror this morning is of starched, pure white professionalism. This is the vision your patients will see every time you go to work from now on. Is this whiteness merely a covering over of a dirty under body? Or is it purity clear through to the soul? Is that bright, fresh, young face a vision born of naivety or dedication to a Christ-like ideal? Your hospital I.D. and it's embossed name tag add the final professional aura to your uniform. Has this picture been a projection of the basics of nursing care well studied, or have you slid through some of your classes by the skin of your teeth so that your foundations are a little shaky?

Revelations 3 speaks of our true position before God on judgment day. We are all imperfect in the backdrop of our Father's requirements for righteousness. We all appear alive and vibrant but can still be spiritually dead.

"Remember, therefore, what you have you have received and heard; obey it. …He who overcomes will, like them, be dressed in white. I will never blot out his name from the book of life…" (Rev. 3:3).

On the first day of clinicals, remember to renew your dedication to serve God in your nursing career as you have in other areas of your life. You will then be truly "Robed in White."

Prayer

Dear Jesus, please walk with me each day on the nursing units, and help me do everything as conscientiously as your righteousness demands. I know you will forgive me if I don't totally succeed in this endeavor because you look at my attitude, rather than my success. I do request your strength, however, to give 100% effort. I love you, Amen.

I.D.'s

"I will write on him the name of my God.... And I will also write on him my new name"
(Rev. 3:12).

One of the least expensive pieces of wardrobe in the hospital, but one that must be worn by every patient, is the identification band. It is cheap plastic and probably costs a few cents, but many things cannot be done without it. The patient who enters the E.R. or admitting office is immediately slapped with a wristband that includes his name, sex, age, doctor, and an identification number. The band is necessary and valuable because no medication doses, lab blood draws, surgeries, or blood transfusions can be administered without checking the I.D. band against the chart record.

Cain killed his brother, Abel. He was moaning because he felt his punishment from God was too severe. He was afraid of being assaulted because he had been driven out from under the protection of his home, family, and God. God had mercy on him and placed a mark on Cain so that no one would dare to harm him. The God of creation gave His I.D. to him for his safety and peace of mind.

The book of Revelation speaks of divergent marks of possession and being written in the Lamb's book of life: marked by "*the name of my God.*" Under the surface of the cognizant world, a perpetual spiritual battle is unfolding between those identified with the mark of the Lamb, who is Jesus Christ, and the mark of the "beast", which is the devil.

Whose identification mark do you bear? In whose infantry are you listed to fight? Does your I.D. band confer upon you the safety and peace of mind that Cain's did? Does it protect you against the harm of wrongful medications that the hospital I.D. gives to patients? You have been "I.D. banded" for this life and for eternity. The choice is only whose name you bear.

Prayer

Please write upon me, Lord, the name of Jesus. I want to fight in the Lord's army. I need the protection and peace of mind that only your mark of approval can bring. I also pray that others will see that I wear your I.D. band. In your son, Jesus' name I speak with you, Amen.

The Student Nurse

Between the spring of being a teenager and the summer of womanhood, there sometimes occurs a stormy but very happy time known as "The Life of a Student Nurse."

Student nurses are found everywhere: underneath, on top of, running past, jumping over, or slithering past patients' beds. Doctors yell at them. Charge nurses criticize them. Mothers worry about them. And patients love them.

A student nurse is courage under her uniform, a smile in white, strength in her stride, endless energy, and the best of young womanhood—a modern Florence Nightingale. Just when she is gaining poise and prestige, she turns green during an autopsy, falls over crutches, drops a lunch tray, becomes preoccupied while assisting a doctor, fills urinals with ice, and loses dentures.

This composite creature drives R.N.s to distraction, eats like a team of hungry interns, and works like the whole nursing staff put together. But to the charge nurse she has the stability of mush, the fleetness of a snail, the mentality of a mule, and is held in one piece by adhesive tape and strained nerves. To the alumni she will never work as hard, make more beds, or scrub more cases than her predecessors.

A student nurse likes days off, boys her own age, the O.R. affiliations, certain doctors, her roommate's pretty clothes, and Mom and Dad. No one else finds more pleasure in straightening a wrinkled sheet or wetting a pair of parched lips. No one else can cram into one little head the course of a disease, the bones comprising the pelvis, what to do when a patient is in shock, how to insert a Dobhof tube at 3 a.m., plus the top ten tunes on the hit parade.

You can criticize a student nurse, but you can't discourage her. You can hurt her feelings but you can't make her quit. She is an example of the American way: a determined and hard-working girl doing her best for school and the hospital, a living symbol of faith and sympathetic care, beauty with a candle in its hand.

Whenever she becomes discouraged, she finds a well of strength in thinking a reward awaits somewhere. For surely some of God's angels wear white uniforms instead of halos and carry medicines instead of harps.[3]

Kaleidoscope

The heavens declare the glory of God; the skies proclaim the work of his hands (Ps. 19:1).

It is a gorgeous fall day. The trees are in their peak of color. Here you see a burst of yellow, there you perceive a flaming orange, and in the midst of it cuts a deep green stand of pines. You have taken a few moments of free time to drink in this unusually warm autumn day. Overhead the sky is a deep blue that never seems to come to an end. The sun is so warm, you are back into your shorts for one of the last few days of this year.

As you walk alone or with a special friend, the words of Psalm 19:1 may come to mind. God has created such a beautiful world for us to live in! He could have made everything just black and white, but His creativity and magnitude demanded that He give us an entire spectrum of colors to enjoy. The creation shows us His love, vibrancy, artistic makeup, and commanding possession and sharing of peace—the peace you feel soaking into your pores with the sun's rays.

Nursing, as any profession or occupation, can be very hectic and tense at times. It demands every ounce of every one of your senses, knowledge, and emotions. A day such as this is such a gift. For a few minutes you can feel what heaven must be like. It has got to be so overpowering to our senses we will hardly be able to take it in. We can say with the psalmist, *"Praise the Lord, O my soul; all my inmost being, praise his holy name"* (Ps 103: 1).

Prayer

Lord, receive my feelings and thoughts about the beauty of this day as an offering of praise to your greatness. Thank you for giving me just one more day of warmth, combined with the various colors of fall, before the snows of winter set in. Your generosity in making my world so beautiful is deeply appreciated. In Jesus' name, Amen.

Work, Work, Work

A man can do nothing better than to eat and drink and find satisfaction in his work. This too, I see, is from the hand of God, for without him, who can eat or find enjoyment? To the man who pleases him, God gives wisdom, knowledge, and happiness... (Eccl. 2:24-26).

Homework questions to answer, five chapters to read, two papers to write, a part-time job to mesh with classes, shopping to be done, laundry to be washed, and you and your roommates just finished making a calendar of which weeks will be yours to clean the bathroom and the dorm room. How will you ever find time to do it all? There just aren't enough minutes in a day, it seems, to get this all accomplished and still eat and sleep. It's unbelievable that summer and its innate times of relaxation are now only three months in the past. Our Bible passage for this week speaks of the endlessness of work, it's seeming meaninglessness from a human point of view and yet, of its importance in pleasing God. So how does God expect you to finish all these tasks?

I, and He, suggest that you do what one employee bulletin board announcement said: "In case of fire, flee the building with the same reckless abandon that occurs each day at quitting time." Flee from your work for a short respite and come apart to your

God in prayer and worship. "How can I do that?" you may say. "I'm already out of time and now you add another thing to my list!" I say this because I have personally found that, when you bring your concerns to the Lord, He will listen, calm your palpitating heart, and then energize your brain with an organizational plan that will allow each task to be accomplished in its appointed time. God's peace of mind will eliminate panic and wasted minutes. The time you spend in communion with God each day will never be wasted. Try it and see.

Prayer

My triune God, please hear my prayer today. Calm my heart and mind, and give me the wisdom, Lord, to accomplish what you have set before me. Clear my thoughts so I can be organized and have no wasted efforts. I want to be able to spend time with you and still do the best I can in my calling as a nursing student. Thank you for hearing and answering my prayer. In Jesus' name, Amen.

Mail Call

I thank my God every time I remember you (Phil. 1:3).

When you were living at home with your little brothers or sisters, did you dream of the time when you could quit babysitting Brenda and Jason, ignore their begging, and never play another board game or computer game with them the rest of your life? Was the Shangri-La of your future a place where you could park your car in the driveway without it being imprinted with the seam lines of Tim's baseball. Did you crave being able to sit down to a whole TV show without Tory pestering you to get off so he and his friends could pay homage to the Nintendo god?

"Where are those ticks of irritation now," you wonder, as your heart lifts and peace sighs through your chest on your way back from the mailbox. The presence of any one of those four names in the return address of the letter you hold in your hand today, seems to have eradicated those old frustrations. You never had an inkling of the value in the contents of that 3" x 3" x 12" box at the Residence Assistant's desk, did you? Now your spirits can rise or fall ninety degrees depending on whether that mailbox is occupied or empty each night when you check it.

News of Tim's baseball team's championship or his personal pitching debut now makes you realize how much you would like to watch one of his games again. Memories of Tory and his two friends cheering or moaning over the point total of Dracula's Revenge curls the corners of your mouth now. Brenda's wide-eyed rapt attention to your past recollections of prom night have blanketed all those lost games of Chutes and Ladders.

How time and distance can change our perspectives! Paul's letters to the Philippian Christians in Asia, God's letter to us in the Bible, and your letters from and to home all contain the same basics which make each one invaluable—love. Love for each other that miles cannot separate, fond memories of past interactions, wishes for your loved one's health, success, and fulfillment, and a longing for resumed experiences in the future are found in all these letters.

On the day you're desperately homesick and yearn to fall back into the security and familiarity of home and family; on the day you miss your siblings' ballgame or band concert to study for a midterm and you're feeling that your career is cheating you out of some of the basic pleasures in life; on the day you walk into the conference room at work at just the wrong time and overhear the staff nurses complain about the trials of "putting up with" the new batch of student nurses; and on the many occasions when the odd working schedule of nursing delays your times with friends—you need to do some reading. Re-read God's letters to you in the Bible and the letters from your family. Both will make you feel deeply loved, fulfilled, and hopeful for your future in nursing.

Prayer

I love and long for time with you, my Lord, and with the people who support me in life and love me. Bless them for loving me and help me to return that love and support. Thank you for teaching me to appreciate my siblings for their value in my life. Forgive me for taking them for granted when I was at home with them and even being impatient with them at times. How I now love your letters to me in the Bible and theirs to me in the mail! In Jesus' name, I ask you to hear my thanks and my confessions, Amen.

Party Time

Do not be deceived: God cannot be mocked. A man reaps what he sows (Gal. 6:7).

"Hi Betsy. This is Shawn from microbiology class."

"Hello Shawn. What can I do for you?"

I guess that sounded fairly calm and nonchalant even though I'm far from it. Shawn is the heartthrob with the haunting blue eyes and body-builder physique who I had spoken with a few times after class. Many times, I had wished he would call and ask me out. Maybe this is the moment! No, probably not. He more than likely just needs a question about microbiology answered.

"I was wondering if you would go with me to a party this Saturday?"

I can't believe this! He's really asking me out! Awesome. Oh my goodness, will Heidi and Karen ever be jealous. "I would love to go with you, Shawn. What time do I need to be ready?"

"I'll be picking you up at 7 p.m. We'll be attending the Phi Beta Kappa Fall Fling. Wear something casual. See you then."

I was right. Heidi and Karen screamed with delight when they heard the news. "You scum! How do you rate? What we would give to be in your position."

Two days later the atmosphere had changed. Someone mentioned that the police were called to the last Phi Beta Kappa party due to disorderly conduct and alcohol use in excess. Rumor has it that Shawn was one of the attendees with an alcohol problem. A few choice questions reveal that next Saturday's party is a B.Y.O.B. affair. This puts my conscience on alert. I think: "Shall I call Shawn and ask him some specific questions? Should I withdraw my acceptance if I get the wrong answers? Will Shawn be furious of being scrutinized? I'll just kick myself over and over if everything is above reproach and Shawn blackballs me because of my suspicions. If it is drinking party, I could just attend and not drink. But what if news about my attendance is the focus of gossip? My reputation could be forever tarnished. But, who cares what other people say? I would be a fool to turn down a date with someone of Shawn's caliber. Maybe I'm making a big deal out of nothing."

In all of Betsy's musings, did you notice anything missing? Anywhere in her reasoning did she include prayer? I find it astounding that prayer is almost always the last thing we do in the decision-making process. Is that because the temptation is so strong we want to hang on to the possibility of indulging without getting burned by the flashback? We suspect that, when we open the decision up to the Lord, the door will shut and be permanently locked. We long to sit on the fence and let temptation tantalize our lives.

So now how does Betsy solve her Shawn problem and how do we handle similar decisions? We need to begin with prayer, continue or start avid Bible reading, and finish with more prayer. Matthew 10:28 tells us not to fear other people but to fear God who can kill both the body and soul. James 1:5 instructs us to ask for wisdom from God to aid us in making our decisions. A good name should be more important than wealth or prestige, Proverbs 22:1 says. In 2 Peter 2:9, God tells us that He knows how to deliver the righteous out of temptation.

We, and Betsy, need to have an honest and open conversation with God and the persons involved in our decision. Then we need to meet our temptations face to face. We can be assured our God will give us wisdom to make the correct decision.

Prayer

Help me to admit, Lord, that I am tempted. Please give me a sensitive conscience, along with righteous wisdom, for making the proper decision. I want to be more concerned with what you think than what other people and Shawn think. In Jesus' name I pray, Amen.

Calorie Counts

May my heart be blameless toward your decrees, that I may not be put to shame (Ps. 119:80).

With advances in care of the cancer patient, AIDS patient, multisystem organ failure patient, and ARDS patient, as well as transplant patients, nutritional therapy has become essential to patient survival. As a student nurse you have been, or will be, involved in tabulating calorie counts and the I & O's of your patient's meals. Administration of TPN or PPN intravenously, nutritional enteral therapy, and PEG tube feedings are an everyday duty of the R.N. in the hospital of today. The severely compromised condition of many inpatients gives us, as nurses, a professional challenge that staff nurses of fifteen years ago never had to deal with because these were the patients who previously expired before leaving the ICU/CCU units. Today, the accuracy of documentation for I & O's, solid food intake, diligence in administering parenteral feedings, speedy insertion of peripheral or central venous I.V. lines, daily weight measurements, and skin turgor evaluations can literally be the ounce that tips the scales for or against your client's prognosis for survival.

Student nurses typically give that extra time and effort to their patients the average staff nurse doesn't have the time or youthful energy to provide given the staffing allocations in most hospitals. Your patients receive what was once the frosting on the cake but now has become the vital physical essential to life's survival. A patient can physically survive if proper nutrition is timely and adequate, but he or she also needs to be nurtured emotionally and spiritually in order to truly survive well. When there is physical stress, there will be emotional and spiritual stresses also. Remember to always give holistic treatment to each of your patients because our total body systems are always intertwined. Treat your patient, not just his or her condition. Sometimes your role will be to provide a quiet, un-intruded place of acceptance and concern so he or she can voice his inner feelings to a non-judgmental listener. You may be asked to contact the pastoral care representative, to read the Bible or Koran to your patient, or pray at his bedside before a procedure or surgery. This will always be in your job description along with your technical expertise.

Just as you are very precise with all your calculations and administrations of physical nutritional therapy, you must also hone your listening skills and your spiritual understanding. Daily personal devotions are as valuable to your nursing technique as procedural videos. Don't neglect prayer and Bible reading in favor of textbook knowledge. Do them both. Also spend time with fellow nurses who love the Lord, so that you can learn from their wisdom and they from yours. Your total patient care therapy must always encompass the physical, spiritual, emotional, and social aspects of your patient's life during illness.

Prayer

Lord, please keep me aware of my own spiritual calorie count. Help me to find the time to adequately feed on your Word. Make me understand that I cannot spiritually or emotionally support my patients if I neglect my personal religious growth or become strung out emotionally in my private life. Keep me balanced, Lord, so that I can truly provide holistic medical care to my patients. In Jesus' name, Amen.

Monkey See: Can Monkey Do?

Pride goes before a fall.… Better to be lowly in spirit …. Whoever gives heed to instruction prospers (Prov. 16:18-20).

Quite a few years back, when I was in nursing school, all the technical aspects of nursing care were either demonstrated in the nursing lab or in the clinical setting on actual patients who were agreeable to allowing several students to watch their treatment. With the onset of MTV, VHS, CDs, and DVDs, videos have hit the classroom. I'm sure that this approach is less embarrassing for the patient, more economical, allows a larger viewing audience, and can more readily be reviewed by individual students. It can, however, cause more anxiety to the beginning student. Explanation of the procedure followed by visualization or hands-on practice has been shown to be more effective in long-term retention of knowledge. You were probably shown several videotaped procedures in the classroom and, because of the nature of your patient assignments, may not get a chance to perform the technique for several weeks. This can lead to loss of the fine points of the technique and raise your level of anxiety when eventually asked to demonstrate the treatment with your instructor looking on.

Now that your anxiety level is building, how do you remember all the details and assist the doctor with expertise and in a timely manner? The routines all seem to be jumbled together in your mind. Just when everything is totally mixed together, you'll be expected to display your skills on a patient, without a mistake, while your instructor peers over your shoulder. Are they trying to make you fail? That is what it feels like sometimes.

The time is ripe for a talk with your Lord. He knows your circumstances and how you are feeling even though your classmates see you as unflustered. Remember, *"Pride goes before a fall.... Better it is to be of a lowly spirit."* Don't be tempted to act like you know what you are doing if you are really totally confused. Listen carefully in class, take notes well, and study them faithfully. If you are confused, take Solomon's advice and humble yourself before your instructor and ask her to talk you through the procedure. Once you have actually done it with your own hands, the knowledge will probably be forever engraved in your mind. Your humility will spare your patient harm, and a truly wise instructor will respect your honesty. You will have prevented an embarrassing blunder which pride could have caused. If your instructor is haughty and makes you feel inadequate, just trust that God will deal with her for her attitude. Continue to believe that you have behaved the way God would want you to. It takes a mature and humble person to let his or her defenses down in trying to do his best for God's glory.

Prayer

Be with me each day during clinicals, Lord, and help me to be honest with myself and humble in my behavior before others. I know that you will work this experience, as well as others, to help me to grow spiritually and professionally. In Jesus' name, Amen.

Who Needs History?

For everything that was written in the past was written to teach us, so that through endurance and the encouragement of the Scriptures we might have hope (Rom. 15:4).

Yesterday the mountaintop, today the valley; why can't everyday be spent in clinicals? There is so much to learn about hundreds of extremely vital nursing procedures. Why do you have to go to history classes too? What do these nonprofessional classes have to do with nursing anyway? What a waste of time and money! All this jumping through hoops just to please the degree requirements and give the college more of your precious paycheck.

We have all had these frustrations in college. We spend hours of time in high school on the basics. Now we want to have tunnel vision focused only on the job that lies ahead. Well, right now history class is what lies ahead. We are part of history, we are making history, and, as Christians, we are commanded to mold history. History class will help you understand life outside of your profession, so you can assist in conforming this world to God. Secondly, you can apply the general principle for studying history to your general approach to nursing. It is said, "We study history so we can be aware of the mistakes and lessons learned by our forefathers, so we don't make the same mistakes." We can build on their lessons learned and try to apply other nurses' successes and failures to our situations today. Be instrumental in pointing to the past so as to not let history repeat itself. And finally, many times we just have to be diligent in the little things in life, so we can be rewarded with the responsibility to impact the great things.

So, don't turn off that alarm, roll over, and go back to sleep. Get up and go to that history class. You'll probably discover some insight you can apply to your future. If not, at least you can be a good steward of the time God has given you today and be responsible even in the hard and boring things of life. This will help you grow, since all of life is going to contain those things that just need to be borne with grace.

Prayer

Holy Spirit, please give me assistance in the area of self-control. I need to be jolted into remembering that service to you starts with diligence in the small and sometimes boring tasks of life. Help me to see what I can apply from history class to my profession. Keep me dedicated and focused. Thank you for the strength you give me each day! Amen.

Saint Christopher

But the eyes of the LORD are on those who fear him… to deliver them from death… he is our help and our shield (Ps. 33:18-20).

In the 1950s and 1960s there was a Catholic religious trend that involved placing a statue of St. Christopher, the patron saint of safety, on the dashboard of your car. The tradition was at times considered synonymous with the proverbial "good-luck charm" concept. Others simply considered it to be a reminder to the passengers that there was danger in automobile transportation that was out of the driver's control, and they needed to add safety in traveling to their prayer list before leaving on a journey.

The level of danger in car pooling to work has not changed appreciably in the six decades since this practice originated, but St. Christopher is no longer perched on our dashboards. We travel between our college campuses and home, between hospital clinicals and the supermarket with seldom a thought to the risks we take every day. We arrogantly assume that accidents will always happen to the other guy until the one day when that oncoming car crosses the centerline and you have that split second to react. You swerve, he jerks his car back into his own lane, and all is silent except for the pounding of your heartbeat in your throat. St. Christopher, your guardian angel, the Lord, or just plain "luck" have been with you again. Life becomes instantly precious and will not be taken for granted for at least the next twenty-four hours. Safety may even be the topic of your prayers for the week following the scare. Then you will inevitably drift back into your coma of complacency.

This scenario is repeated over and over again in our lives with only the alteration of plot changing the focus. What a comfort to know that God's "eye is upon us" and he is "our shield." Whether the scenario includes physical, spiritual, or emotional danger, we can be assured that God cares and God controls. That is a given substance in this equation. Each equation has two sides though. We need to remember that our side of that equation involves "lifting up our eyes to the hills." We need to be more aware of the many things God controls for us and around us. We need to prod ourselves into more prayers of gratitude for God's basic provisions in life. What happens to us each day is not a matter of "good luck."

Prayer

I do not need St. Christopher for my protection or as my intercessor, Lord Jesus. I acknowledge you as creator, controller, and protector. Thank you for demonstrating your love for me in this way also. I will try to be more mindful of the good things that occur every day of my life because of your care, Amen.

Home Sweet Home

Like a bird that strays from its nest is a man who strays from home (Prov. 27:8).

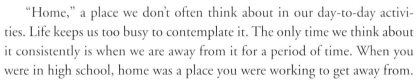

"Home," a place we don't often think about in our day-to-day activities. Life keeps us too busy to contemplate it. The only time we think about it consistently is when we are away from it for a period of time. When you were in high school, home was a place you were working to get away from. As you thought about college, one of your many reasons for attending was to get away from home, out on your own, to be your own boss. In contrast, patients in the hospital have a constant desire to return home. Every day is measured by how soon they will get home again. Now that you are "on your own" at college you can probably understand your patient's longing a little better. For most of us home represents loving relationships, shared feelings, safety and protection. A concrete place where people care enough to help one another and love enough to forgive. You've maybe found out that a large college campus can be a very threatening place at times both physically and emotionally. The feelings you shared at home can be met with derision in your dorm room. Professors

61

often seen motivated to see how difficult they can make their subject rather than being concerned about how well they can help you understand the material. Failing a certain percentage of their students each term is a verbalized goal some of them have. The home you wanted to leave so badly a few months ago, you are now homesick for. How you yearn to have big sister around to help with a decision. How nice it would be to have Dad pay the phone bill you just received. It would be wonderful to just sit down to homework once again while Mom did the laundry. Many things in our lives are only fully appreciated when we have left them behind or lost them permanently.

The Bible has many references to home also. It is a valued place we are permitted to long for (Deut. 24:5, Ps. 4:3). Home is a place of safety and security (Ruth 1:11). Proverbs 3:33 and 2 Chronicles 16:43 depict home as a place where blessings flow out of loving relationships. If we are Christians, then God promises us a home in heaven someday. A home He has specially prepared for us with all the features we now miss (John 14:1-4). Even God himself longed for home and in 2 Samuel 7:1-16 he tells David, through Nathan the prophet, to build him a place of cedar to call home. He acknowledges the human need to be at home where one can rest from his enemies.

What I am trying to say is, your homesickness is not unusual, nor should it be unexpected. God understands your feelings. You can speak freely to Him about your concerns and fears, and ask for His strength to overcome. You certainly now appreciate so many things you once took for granted. Let the people you miss know how much they mean to you and even how homesick you are right now, so they can be supportive. So when you "get a minute," call home. When you get a day, go home. Isn't it wonderful that home is a place where the door will always be open. If that is not true of your home on earth, it will be of your home in heaven.

Prayer

Thank you, Lord, for helping me see the value of home and family. Thank you also for understanding my loneliness. Please help me to voice my appreciation to my family for their support and to make my campus a home away from home. Because you are always here with me, I am never truly alone, and your strength will see me through yet another hurdle of life. In Jesus' name, Amen.

Pride Comes Before a Fall

Do not keep talking so proudly or let your mouth speak such arrogance, for the LORD is a God who knows, and by him deeds are weighed (1 Sam. 2:3).

"I would like to explain the rationale for the tests and treatments you are receiving, Mr. Williams. I'm sure that Mary has said many things about them which were helpful but could not possibly have given you a complete understanding of what is about to occur. She is only a student nurse and is still learning, so you cannot expect her to know as much about the value of patient teaching as a veteran nurse like myself. I am Mary's instructor. The test you will be having this afternoon will help us determine if there are any ulcers in your stomach."

"Yes, I know. Mary explained that to me."

"Oh, well good. The procedure will involve the use of a flexible tube which the doctor will place through your esophagus and into your stomach."

"Yes, I know. Mary has explained the whole procedure to me."

"Do you have any further questions you would like to ask?"

"No, I feel well prepared."

The instructor quickly and humbly exited the room.

The scene may be slightly different than the one I depicted but we have all had times when our instructor, a doctor, or a colleague, have pridefully determined that they possess so much more knowledge than we do. They have then proceeded to condescendingly impart that knowledge to us or to our patients. What a frustrating and humiliating scene! Fortunately for Mary, her patient had the courage to speak up on her behalf and even praise her work. Her instructor's pride was quickly pricked. Hopefully, she learned a lesson from the patient and her student. Pride can be such a temptation for all of us! How often do we assist a patient with something just because we want him or her to think we are a "good nurse"? How often have you spewed technical jargon at a patient hoping to have your patient think that you are very knowledgeable? We want our patients and friends to have confidence in our abilities, so we spout medical terms as a smoke screen to help them think we know exactly what we are doing when we really need more in-depth knowledge in order to be truly instructive?

We need to remember always to be humbly honest with all people, especially our patients. This will likely spare us the embarrassment of instructors or doctors who try to one-up us. Admit when you can't thoroughly answer a question, ask your colleagues' opinions, and/or search out the correct answer in your textbook in an effort to be totally honest and accurate in your replies. As Christians, we need to acknowledge other nurse's good techniques and then be humble enough to learn from their example. We all desire to be excellent nurses, so avoid false pride, keep the patient's welfare above all else, and follow Jesus' example of being a humble servant, always placing the advancement of others above your own. Remember what the Bible says in 1 Samuel 2:3: *Do not keep talking so proudly or let your mouth speak such arrogance, for the* Lord *is a God who knows, and by him deeds are weighed."*

Prayer

Please help me, Lord, to be more concerned about how you weigh my actions and motives, then what other people may think of me. Forgive me for the times, in the recent past, when I may have fudged my words in an attempt to impress others. Help me to be humble and honest in all my dealings with my patients and colleagues. I pray for the insight of your Holy Spirit to let me know when I am exaggerating or being prideful. In Jesus' name, and in the knowledge that His sacrifice has made me right with you, Amen.

Leave the Lights On

Do not let your hearts be troubled. Trust in God; trust also in me. In my Father's house are many rooms.... I am going there to prepare a place for you (John 14:1-2).

I've had an unsettled day on the nursing unit today and am feeling a little insecure. When I feel this way, my thoughts go back to more secure times at my parents' home. My parents' home sits nestled in one of the safest neighborhoods I know. It is perched midway down a "No Outlet" road with access to only two cross streets. Ever since I was old enough to stay out later than the sun, my parents left the lights on, outside of our garage, until every family member was home for the night. Though I forgot on numerous occasions to turn them off when I was the last one home, they were always shining brightly every time I rounded the last corner of our road. Even today, when my siblings or I notify our parents that we will be coming for a visit, those garage lights are once again left on till we arrive. Those spots of light in the darkness of night are still warm and welcome reminders that someone inside is expecting me and cares about me.

Jesus too, waits for us His children to return to Him. Let's face it, some of us are staying out pretty late. Nevertheless, Jesus' lights are always on: the light of His gospels, the light of the preached word, and the light of his childrens' examples. Our verses for this week tell us to let our lights shine for the people of our world so they may also be welcomed and secure because of the light. The verses in John 14 also inform us that Jesus has gone to heaven ahead of us, having risen from the grave, and is preparing a place for us at His estate.

As nurses, we have a unique opportunity to be Jesus' lights to our patients. We are by their sides during their most vulnerable moments. When they grasp for a bit of hope, reach for comfort, and nearly explode with joy, we are there. We can shine Jesus' light in words, in deeds, and in acts of love and concern. We do not preach; we model Jesus' example. We do not push; we give them options to choose. We do not judge; we accept each one as equally valuable to Jesus. Now that is security![4]

Prayer

Lord, help me be a light for you in times of joy, sorrow, and hopelessness. Show your people, who are staying away from you for so long, the way to salvation through Jesus' death on the cross, His rising from the grave, and His ascension into heaven. Let them know that you love them through your words in the Bible, through preaching they may hear on the radio, TV, or by attending a church service, and my example of Christ-like love and concern. Show these new children of yours the way to the home prepared for them in heaven. Let them know you are waiting for them with the lights left on. In Jesus' name, Amen.

Never Alone

Have I not commanded you? Be strong and courageous. Do not be terrified; do not be discouraged, for the LORD your God will be with you wherever you go (Josh. 1:9).

My hands shook so hard I couldn't believe they were mine. This was my first attempt at giving a "shot" to an actual patient. I carefully drew up the heparin from the tiny vile and tapped the syringe to remove the inevitable bubble forming inside. Slowly drawing the safety cap over the needle, I grabbed the alcohol wipes and entered my patient's hospital room. With my instructor in tow, I pinched the area of my patient's abdomen which I had just wiped clean with the alcohol swab. While saying, "Here goes a little poke," I directed the needle at the proper angle toward her belly. The needle bounced! Horrified, I looked toward my instructor who promptly left to get me a new sterile needle with which to try again. I changed needles and on this second try it went in smoothly. With a quick voicing of sorrow to my patient, and in a flourish of red-hot blush moving rapidly up my face, I left the room. My instructor simply smiled and said, "It happens. You just wanted to avoid hurting your patient so you did not apply enough tension to the poke." One of my fellow students, seeing the look on my face, asked what was wrong. I explained my "tragedy," to which she surprisingly replied, "Me too."

During the course of my nurses' training I will assuredly have technique and decision-making mistakes, which will be decidedly of more consequence. This was merely my first and therefore, will always stand out in my mind. I was reminded once again that I am just as human as the next person and cannot expect myself to be perfect. My instructor's comment was right on the mark. I need to learn the balance between being kind to my patient and yet doing an effective job of performing the procedure needed to bring long term healing to her.

The verses we are studying this week have several applications to this situation. First of all, notice the non-judgmental response of my instructor and the supportive statement of my fellow student. They definitely displayed the loving response that Hebrews 13 mentions. Secondly, it calls to our attention the promises our Lord makes to us in His Bible: *"Never will I leave you; never will I forsake you."* I could feel God's presence with me, helping me to go ahead with the hypodermic injection even though my hands were trembling. Thirdly, God was my helper when I was required to attempt the insertion a second time. I was fearful and embarrassed, but He still gave me the help to not be overcome by my humiliation. Then He assisted me in the procedure, so I could then be successful. Finally, He showed me that, not only was He with me for the incident, as He will be in the future, but He also gave me human support.

Prayer

Dear Father in heaven, no matter what happens in my life for either good or ill, I know you will be there with me. I ask for your help in forgiving myself for this little mistake. Help me to keep all things in perspective. Bless those who supported me with their loving statements. Give me the love and commitment to share this same support with others in the future. Thank you for not only being with me in a nebulous way but also in a concrete way through the support of my colleagues. In Jesus' name, Amen.

Deep Cleaned

Let us draw near to God with a sincere heart in full assurance of faith, having our hearts sprinkled to cleanse us from a guilty conscience… (Heb. 10:22).

Butler Cleaners, "The cleaner people"; Grand Highlands, "Steam cleaned is deep cleaned"; Magic Dry, "We don't cut corners, we clean them." "Cleanliness is next to godliness."

Everyone knows the value of cleanliness. Everyone also knows the repulsions associated with the smells and sights we are subjected to when we are in the presence of someone or something unclean. Clean techniques and universal precautions are the foundation of every task we perform as members of the medical profession. Remember the many ways that our hospitals reinforce hand washing diligence and the need to use gloves with all procedures that involve contact with body fluids.

Our lives as Christians have been cleansed from all sin by the blood of Jesus (1 John 1:7). We strive to walk in His light and in fellowship with one another, but are we ever 100% clean? Just as our steam-cleaned carpet is clean on the surface but contains an amazing amount of dirt next to it's backing, we know in our hearts that we are not totally pure and above condemnation. We don't shoplift, but we do take gloves, or hemostats, or ink pens home from the hospital with us. This is a breakage of the commandment not to steal. We don't habitually lie, but we have all reported post-op vitals as having been completed when we didn't actually have time to do every one of those "every fifteen-minute check-ups." This is indeed a breakage of the commandment to not bear false witness. We have all "*sinned and fall short of the glory of God*" (Rom. 3: 23). In ourselves, we will never be 100% clean in accordance with God's sense of justice. We cannot be perfect and therefore are unclean.

Our verse in Hebrews for this week tells us that though we can't become clean in our own strength, with faith in God, we can become totally cleansed. Therefore, let us admit that we need assistance to become morally clean, that God the Father has provided that assistance in the form of his son, Jesus, and that all we need to do is accept this free gift of cleansing by faith in Christ's sacrifice for us on the cross.

God's holiness requires perfection. Our mistakes and errors in judgment are as repulsive a stench in our Lord's nostrils as the body smells emitted from a street person turn our stomachs as we try to give comprehensive health care to him. It will take many wheelchair showers to remove these smells from his body. We, however, can be instantly cleansed from our sins by belief in Jesus as our own personal savior. Praise the Lord. We are indeed deep cleaned!

Prayer

Lord Jesus, thank you for dying for my "little" sins that no one else knows anything about. Thank you, Holy Spirit, for making me aware of my uncleanness. And, Father in heaven, please accept the purity Jesus has earned for me on the cross. I strive to live in your light. Please help me to scrub out more and more of these secret sins as well as my blatant ones, Amen.

The Green Dragon

Anger is cruel and fury is overwhelming, but who can stand before jealousy? (Prov. 27:4).

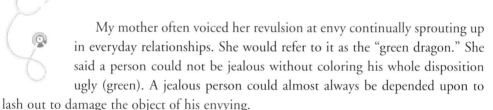

My mother often voiced her revulsion at envy continually sprouting up in everyday relationships. She would refer to it as the "green dragon." She said a person could not be jealous without coloring his whole disposition ugly (green). A jealous person could almost always be depended upon to lash out to damage the object of his envying.

Joseph's story of being sold into slavery by his brothers (Gen. 37) is the Bible's classic example of unrestrained jealousy to the extreme. It was also envy that Jesus blamed for His eventual death. The chief priests couldn't tolerate losing face or being stripped of some of their power, so they arranged for Jesus' demise.

We nurses are always embroiled in relationships with people. Instances of jealousy can occur daily. When you study four hours for your medical-surgical test and your roommate studies two hours, but she gets an A- and you get a C, jealousy can rear its head. When your hands are trembling as you assist the doctor with a lumbar puncture and the next day your classmate glows with confidence and perfection in the same situation, comparisons will be made. When the young man who's been walking with you to physiology class asks your high-school acquaintance out to a movie instead of you, anger may arise. Jealousy will be there to cloud your judgments often, in many different circumstances.

Titus 3:1-8 gives us all a very appropriate way to deal with this sin, which will never actually be totally avoided. It says, *"We lived in malice and envy, being hated and hating one another."* This is referring to our relationship quotient when we were yet unsaved. Think of an occurrence of jealousy in your own life. Did it provoke anger and even some hatred of the person who "showed you up"? Often, either someone is "ticked off" because you accomplished something or possess some trait he desires, or you are angry with someone else because she got the glory that you think you deserve. Jealousy is with us all. What can we do about it? Titus 3 gives us the solution. Because God, in His love and mercy saved us though we were unrighteous, we can live in kindness and love toward others. If we lean on God for help, we can *"devote ourselves to doing what is good. These things are excellent and profitable for everyone."*

Jealousy equals hatred and anger. Love equals kindness to those we hate or those who hate us. Then we can let our God be the promoter of all successes, the rewarder of our humility, and squelcher of any pride that may cause the "green dragon" of jealousy to rise against us.

Prayer

I admit, Lord, that jealousy is part of my life. Please do not let it overpower me so that I become hateful and revengeful. I will speak with you when it occurs and I ask for your strength to turn my jealousy into love. I know from your Word that you see all people as equal when justified by your grace. Help me to humbly be what you have called me to be, while letting others use their personal talents for your service without any comparison of gifts. And, if it be your will, may I even learn to revel in the successes of others. In Jesus' name, Amen.

Gravity

Just as Moses lifted up the snake in the desert, so the Son of Man must be lifted up, that everyone who believes in him may have eternal life (John 3:14-15).

What a fantastic concept gravity is. Astronauts do experiment after experiment studying the effects of the lack of it. Everyday life would be extremely complicated and even dangerous without it. Our profession depends on gravity in some very intricate ways in technology, but I.V. infusion is probably its simplest form and the most frequently used. Everyday at least fifty percent of the patients on any given unit will have an I.V. running. Some will be placed on an infusion pump but many will just flow by gravity. What happens when you place an I.V. bag below the level of your patient's needle site? The person's blood flows back into the tubing and I.V. fluid is pushed back into the drip chamber. If the bag is at the same level as the entrance site, no flow is allowed unless you have a pump to force the flow. If it is placed on an I.V. pole above the patient's bed it will run in rapidly, giving life-sustaining nourishment, electrolytes, and any necessary antibiotics. Gravity is fantastic! Gravity is essential.

When I read Numbers 21:9, I pictured an I.V. setup. Jesus and the serpent were both lifted up on a pole. That lifting up process symbolized a life-saving event in the lives of everyone connected to the object being elevated. When the Israelites believed that looking upon the serpent could save them from physical death after having been bitten, they were indeed saved from dying. When we make a decision to believe that Jesus died on the cross to save us from our sins, we receive spiritual life.

The next time you administer an I.V., remember your Savior's death on the cross for you. Stay connected to Him and remain "in-line" with the life sustaining spiritual food He can give you. If you place your plans above the Lord's leading, you will push back the spiritual food you need to live eternally. If you coast through life resting on your original profession of faith but never delving into the Word of God, spiritual nourishment will come to a standstill and you will miss the joy of growth. But, if you stay connected to Jesus, seek His wisdom in your life's decisions, and seek to remain "in-line" with His spiritual nourishment, you can benefit from "spiritual" gravity.

Prayer

Tonight I have received a spiritual infusion from your Word, Lord. Thank you for that Word, the Bible. I look to you, Lord Jesus, for my salvation. I seek the power of your Holy Spirit to apply your Word and salvation toward my spiritual growth. Please help me to renew my spiritual I.V.s daily, Amen.

God's Billboards

Faith comes from hearing the message, and the message is heard through the word of Christ
(Rom. 10:17).

The epitome of servanthood to Jesus, Paul, the Pharisee of Pharisees, who was blinded physically so that his soul could finally see God, this is our biblical example of zeal and single-mindedness for bringing the gospel of peace to the world.

When you look at our title for this week and read about Paul, you may think, "Oh, no, another devotional to make me feel guilty because I'm supposed to be witnessing and focused, but I'm not matching up!" Not!

Are you a Christian? Do you try to do what you believe God wants you to do? Are you working hard to get along with your fellow classmates, your dorm partners, and the nursing staff on your assigned unit? Do you talk with your God and seek His leading in decisions you make? Then your life is on God's track. You may not be perfect in your service of Him, but your motives are pure. God sees that your attitude is one of service to Him.

Compare yourself with non-Christians your own age, not old Paul. Yes, I said, "compare." You will find that you are different because your focus in life is stable and directed, not blown around by each new fad. When you finish your rotation or get a reading recess, do you hang it all up or manufacture a hangover rather than studying or doing that reading? Probably not. Then, yes, you are showing the world your values. You are witnessing. Unless God has stopped you in your tracks, like Paul, or made your inner spirit ill at ease until you follow a specific path in life as many ministers and missionaries attest, let your lifestyle be your witness. God wants us to bring a message of peace to a frantic world. When you can be at peace, hopeful, and contented even though you're studying 24/7, you're above the bill of your cap in debt, and the hospital staff is being impatient with your inexperienced assistance because you are still unorganized at your trade, you are spreading God's attitude to the world. Letting God own and direct you as you persevere in your learning, will manifest to others the security and love you have at the foundation of your life. God's love does not lay guilt trips. That thought pattern comes from His enemy. You are God's billboard to a population that feels lost and confused more often than they care to admit. With a desire for His leadership, a willingness to obey His directions, and some spiritual aging, you too will be able to someday be His spokesman along with your lifestyle witnessing. *Shalom!*

Prayer

Father, I have felt pushed and guilty many times when I have been terrified to open my mouth in full-blown witness of my love for you. I have wished so many times that I could have spoken to patients and/or colleagues, at the right time, the words that came into my mind two hours later. What a relief to know that you understand me so well that your love takes into account my attitudes rather then my rhetoric. That, as my heavenly Father, you patiently wait for me to mature spiritually, knowing that I will then be able to also speak out for you as Paul did many centuries ago. In Jesus' name, Amen.

Fearful But Not Faltering

Have no fear of sudden disaster or of the ruin that overtakes the wicked, for the Lord will be your confidence… (Prov. 3:25-26).

One day in July, a farmer sat in front of his ramshackle farmhouse, smoking his pipe, and watching his neighbor plant his corn seed. A stranger came along and asked him, "How's your alfalfa coming?"

"Ain't got any," was the answer.

"Well, how are your soybeans producing?"

"Didn't plant any…'fraid of the drought."

"How about your potatoes?"

"Ain't planted 'em. I was scared of the old 'tater' bugs."

The stranger finally asked, "Well, what did you plant?"

"Nothin'," answered the farmer. "I just played it safe."[5]

Have you ever felt like doing what that farmer did? Just playing it safe and quitting this college scene? Have you ever been fearful of failing, or worse yet, being told to quit because you just aren't hacking it? Did those feelings crop up in microbiology class when you got that D+ after studying so hard, just because the professor took sixty percent of her questions from the captions under the pictures rather than all the data you were told to study? Or maybe it was during one day on the clinical unit when your patient misunderstood your explanation and embarrassed you in front of your instructor by inaccurately telling him what she thought you had said? I can understand that those types of feelings would come up for you because there were several times during my student nurse days when either I, or my roommates, had to talk each other out of just hanging up our stethoscopes and moving on to another less-demanding occupation. Been there and done that.

Take a moment to put everything into perspective. Why did you choose nursing for your profession? How many times have you had excellent grades on previous tests? What about those patients who have complimented you for the wonderful care you gave them? Will it matter in the years to come if you know all the fine print under the pictures in the book? Haven't you been embarrassed before and survived it just fine? Being a registered nurse is what you felt called by God to be. You have studied diligently and learned so much already. Helping a patient to feel less anxious or less painful has been so fulfilling in the past. Be confident of your "calling" and do the best you know how to do. This is all anyone can reasonably expect from you. Remember, above all else, you are not the only one who has felt this way. Feelings will wax and wane but success usually comes through perseverance. Our texts for this week refer to spiritual perseverance but can be applied to everyday obstacles also.

Prayer

Dear Jesus, I have learned a mountain of information thus far in nurses' training. I will seek to integrate what I have learned to benefit each of my patients. Please give me the wisdom to do that effectively, Lord. In the next few hours, assist me in putting all that has happened to me lately into perspective. I truly enjoy serving in this profession, feel that I was called to this job, and want to stay the course. Holy Spirit, give me insight and strength to continue, Amen.

I Saw Him Again Today

Though the mountains be shaken and the hills be removed, yet my unfailing love for you will not be shaken… (Isa. 54:10).

Why is it that when you love someone you see him everywhere? I saw him again today—the one. I suppose the adjective may sound funny for a man, but he was beautiful. I just can't help thinking about him. He is so sensitive and thoughtful. The best part, however, is that he loves me too. I see so many of my peers chasing around trying to find love, but it is never returned. That's why I feel especially lucky. He's perfect; that's all there is to it. He is 100% faithful to me. He would never hurt me or leave me. I know because he told me so and he has never lied to me. I have to smile just thinking about him. I can't believe anyone can love me the way he does. He sacrifices so much for me. I have a bit of a temper and I've said things to him I regretted later, but he just forgives me and goes on. No matter how often or how badly I hurt him, he just keeps on loving me and giving me another chance—unbelievable! I wish I could say the same for myself but unfortunately, when I'm angry with him, I'm not always so patient. And romantic? He's shown me sunsets and warm starry nights that can't be matched. He's given me every flower known to man, one bouquet after another in breathtaking arrays of color. He always walks with me on sunny afternoons and sits for hours just letting me talk to him…or cry while he gently holds me.

He's constantly sensitive to my needs, always making sure I'm doing okay financially, emotionally, and physically. He'll go with me wherever I want to go, and he's always concerned that I get home safely. Sometimes, it's hard for me to believe someone so selfless could be so real. He's wonderful! He's even concerned about how my friends are doing, and he loves my family. Most importantly, he's a Christian!

If I had one wish, I'd wish everyone could have a love like the one I've found; it fills you, it's exhilarating. You know, he knows a lot of people; I wonder if you have met him. If not, let me introduce you to him. His name is Jesus.[6]

Prayer

"Jesus is all the world to me, my life, my joy, my all. He is my strength from day to day, without him I would fall. When I am sad, to him I go, no other one can cheer me so. He's my friend."[7]

In the words of this song, I voice my convictions, Lord. I need your love, receive your love, and install your love in my everyday life. Words can never express my gratitude to you for giving it to me so generously. I will lean on it today and let it strengthen me in all that I do as a nurse in training. Love always and forever, Amen.

Terror

Have no fear of sudden disaster or of the ruin that overtakes the wicked, for the LORD will be your confidence and will keep your foot from being snared (Prov. 3:25-26).

It was 1900 on the 3-11 p.m. shift and family visiting hours were in full swing on the unit I was assigned to that night. Supper trays were checked for I & O's and I was hanging my last 1800 I.V. piggybacks a little late, as my instructor watched my technique. Suddenly, a furious scuffling punctured the buzz of conversation in every room of the East hall. Mixed with this sound was a forceful, unrelenting, pounding sound that seemed to shake the wall adjacent to our room. Swearing, angry shouts, and a woman's whimpering shattered the calm. Three seconds of catatonic shock passed as nurse Evans and I searched each other's eyes. A mad dash into the hall followed. Crumpled on the floor lay a young woman, her face to the carpet, her right arm protecting the back of her head, and her left arm yanked behind her back. Our "612 patient" was hovering over her, wrenching her arm behind her back, and beating her body with hateful blows wherever he could land a punch. His gown had been left at the bedside with the I.V. line he had pulled apart. Blood was splattering the walls, carpet, and anyone near by with each flail of his fist. Visitors and other patients peeked out of room doorways. Everyone's fright and flight mechanism was instantaneously activated.

"How do we stop this without becoming a victim? Call the security guards! Grab your gloves." My mind was racing. "Where do we grab his body to stop the action? Will we be strong enough to hold his fury in check or will we become the brunt off his knuckles?" The guards came just as we heard the chilling crack of the bone breaking in the young woman's left arm. "Don't stop, but do think and act! Don't let the blood contaminate your eyes or mouth as you help to get him back to his bed. Watch out for those flying arms. Wow, is he strong!"

This was my moment of ultimate fear. If only it were not my patient, I could just step back and watch someone else handle it all.

What would your reaction have been? What thoughts would have sped through your brain? I admit that my situation was extremely rare but you will undoubtedly have your own moment of fear, maybe at your first cardiac arrest or your first experience in the E.R.

My devotions at 0100 that night were concentrated on the texts listed above and also on 2 Timothy 1:7: *"For God did not give us a spirit of timidity, but a spirit of power, of love, and of self-discipline."* God had truly given me power and sound judgment when Ms. Evans, I, and the security guards donned our gloves before returning my distraught patient to his bed. Every word we spoke to him seemed to calm him more. Looking back, I gave God a "thank you" for helping me say the right words at the right time!

It was 0130 and I still couldn't sleep. I "accidentally" opened my Bible to Isaiah 41: 10: *"So do not fear, for I am with you; be not dismayed, for I am your God. I will strength-*

en you and help you; I will uphold you with my righteous right hand." I asked God to apply these words to my troubled heart and was then able to fall asleep peacefully. I would recommend that you memorize one or all of these verses. They will be a comfort to you in those times in nursing when your heart is palpitating at 160 beats per minute.

Prayer

Thank you, Father, for clearing my head, strengthening my muscles, directing my tongue, and upholding me in this crisis! I can hardly believe how I remembered to get my gloves and thought to wait for the guards when my first instinct was to charge in and just help that poor woman. Lord, please heal her of her physical and emotional wounds of tonight. Also bring counselors who are wise in you to assist this man in anger management. In Jesus' name I pray, Amen.

I Quit!

Take up your positions; stand firm and see the deliverance the LORD *will give you. Do not be afraid; do not be discouraged. Go out to face them tomorrow, and the* LORD *will be with you* (2 Chron. 20:17).

It's another one of those all-too-frequent bleak days in March. Everything is wet and cold and the sky is overcast. "How appropriate," you think! It's the middle of second semester, the instructors are cranky, and there is no end to the pile of homework, care plans, and papers to be done for class in the next two weeks. Your mood fits the weather, and the two combined are almost too much to bear. You ask yourself, "Why am I toughing this out? Why don't I just quit?" Many of your friends are working at well-paying jobs and never have to contend with homework. This college life seems worthless and burdensome, and now even the sun refuses to shine!

Take courage. Your feelings are not strange. In our Scripture passage for this week, the great prophet, Elijah, also experienced discouragement and depression, so much so that he not only wanted to quit, but even to die. So do as Elijah did, talk to your Lord and tell him your problems. Trust that He cares about your circumstances. God sent an angel to physically nourish Elijah. God's concern for him gave Elijah strength to go on.

If nursing is what God has led you to pursue, He will strengthen your resolve even as He did for Elijah. You will feel the Father's emotional nourishment, if only you continue to communicate your feelings to Him.

When things go wrong, as they sometimes will,
When the road you're trudging seems all-uphill,
When the funds are low, and the debts are high.
And you want to smile but you have to sigh,
When care is pressing you down a bit,
Rest if you must, but don't you quit!

Life is queer with its' twists and turns,
As everyone of us sometimes learns,
And many a failure turns about,
When he might have won had he stuck it out.
Don't give up though the pace seems slow,
You may succeed with another blow.

Success is failure turned inside out,
The silver tint of the clouds of doubt,
And you never can tell how close you are,
It may be near when it seems so far.
So stick to the fight when you're hardest hit,
It's when things seem worst,
That you must not quit![8]

Prayer

Please show me, Holy Spirit, that I have truly been called to this profession. Help me to focus on your vision for my life and not on your vision for my friends. Dear Jesus, walk with me through my studies and my clinicals so that I can make your example of perseverance in an assigned task, my own. Father God, I thank you once again for loving me enough to give me a great purpose in life. I will not quit if you will be my guide. In Jesus' name, Amen.

Christian Nursing

We will dry tears of pain
With a hand gentle, soft
We will melt walls of fear
Bringing smiles aloft.
We will bring faith and courage
To the broken and scoffed.

We will turn with the hands
Of our father above,
We will comfort with voices
Of Lord Jesus his son.
We'll inspire with the hope
Which from his spirit comes.

We will cradle the infants
With a heart strong and warm.
We will heal with the wisdom
That from heaven is born.
We will hold each frail hand
Until the dying are home

And they'll know we are nurses
By our clothes white as doves.
But they'll know we are Christians
By our love, by our love.
Yes, they'll know we are Christians
By our love.[9]

Tami Seif-Pothoven[10]

Life Goes On

Before the mountains were born or you brought forth the earth and the world, from ever-lasting to everlasting you are God.... For a thousand years in your sight are like a day that has just gone by or like a watch in the night.... The length of our days is seventy years or eighty, if we have the strength.... Teach us to number our days aright, that we may gain a heart of wisdom (Ps. 90:2,4,10,12).

I have lost both my dear father and mother in death at a very elderly age of eighty-seven years and eighty-nine years, respectively, but all of my other close family members are still living as well as all of my wonderful friends. After working in the hospital, however, I am keenly aware of how many families have close relatives whose lives are cut drastically short either by disease or accident. I've stood with families whose loved one is failing. I've even held patients as they took their last breaths. How hard it is on the families who are left behind! Their whole lives need to be reorganized, against their will, around the missing son, husband, father, or grandfather. I've seen the rocky road traveled many times by my friends who have lost loved ones. It's such a small comfort to say life goes on, and yet it must. For some reason, the sleeping family member is finished with his time on earth whether he is two or eighty-two years of age. We can never understand the reasons for the timing of individual lives, so there is futility in trying to explain it. God has a plan for the number of our days even before we are born, as it says in Psalm 139. How wonderful to know that our God cares for all the minute details of our lives. We need not worry about whether we can go on. He will give us all the strength we need to do just that. Our only concern needs to be the diligence we give to the work set before us during our own life span. This takes the terror and the questioning out of life's circumstances for me. It keeps me focused on the race set before me. It helps me comfort a patient's family as they prepare for his imminent death. It decreases my anxiety when I see people my own age or even younger who have died. I know that my days on earth will not end until God has ordained them to do so. I can then strive to fill each of these days full of service to God and to my fellow man. Nursing gives me a wonderful environment to do just that. I thank the Lord for giving me this profession with which to fill my days.

Prayer

Father, I won't ever forget those who have gone before me, but help me not to dwell on my sorrows or the sorrows of my patients' families. Please help me to diligently do the work you have prepared for me to do while I have life to do it. My life is such a small part of your entire plan for human existence, but your word tells me that all I do is vitally important to you! You are such an awesome God! Guide me Father through my place in time I pray. In Jesus' name, Amen.

God's Provision

Do not worry, saying, "What shall we eat?" or "What shall we drink?" or "What shall we wear?"…your heavenly Father knows that you need them (Matt. 6:31-32).

Here we are back to Psalm 104 again. This is a psalm that has been so rich in meaning to me this year, I had to draw you back into it one more time.

God's provision for all His creatures is so obvious in this world if we just take the time, as the psalmist did, to stop and contemplate it. Psalm 104 shows us God's power, majesty, splendor, and intelligence in verses 1-9. His ongoing control of creation is laid out in this first section of the psalm. Verses 10-30 speak of His wise intertwining of plants, animals, and man's existence and how our fatherly and compassionate God provides food and security for every living thing.

So why are we distraught at times when grocery or department store shopping? We just got paid but the check just won't cover all the things we "need." If you buy groceries and gas, then you have nothing left for that new pair of jeans that just went on sale. You can only work a few hours a week between classes, clinical, and studying, so the money just never seems to cover everything. Samuel Butler once said, "All progress is based upon a universal innate desire on the part of every organism to live beyond its income."[11] How true!

When grocery-shopping day comes, we need to change our focus to the focus of the psalmist in verses 31-35 of Psalm 104. We need to praise our Lord for His care for us. We need to be thankful for the money we have garnered. We need to sing to the Lord every day of our lives in all situations. Then God will give us the wisdom to decipher what we need from what we want. We will be at peace with our decisions. Happy shopping!

Prayer

Praise the Lord, oh my soul! Thank you great creator God for the rhythmic world you have called into being. I praise your name for how you provide for me daily. Help me to seek your praise and glory above all material things so I may live in contentment and peace. In your son Jesus' name, who embodied that peace and contentment so nobly, Amen.

The Art of Listening

The LORD came and stood there, calling as at the other times, "Samuel, Samuel." Then Samuel said, "Speak, for your servant is listening" (1 Sam. 3:10).

Our environment today, with all its advances in technology, is so bombarded with sounds! Every second of every day can be full of communication. The radio, the television, C.D. players, telephones, friends, family, preachers, instructors, fellow workers, and patients all vie for our ears. The noise level can tune out all silence if we allow it to do so. The art of listening is becoming a dying art. Every voice and venue demands to be heard above one another.

We need to develop our listening skills as Samuel had done in the Old Testament. If we are to hear what the Lord feels is necessary, we must take time to listen for His voice. Henri Nouwen said, "Somewhere we know that without silence, words lose their meaning, that without listening, speaking no longer heals, that without distance, closeness cannot cure."[12]

As a student nurse with only one or two patients to care for, you will sometimes have extra time to spare. I hope you will use that time to just listen to your patients. I hope you will dedicate yourself to adding the art of listening to your professional "quiver" of techniques. Just knowing that someone cares enough to listen can relieve many fears, concerns, and actual physical and emotional pain. This listening is an active process, not just a passive, distracted presence. Your patient needs to know that the people attending to her healing, care enough to close out all of the world's noise and time pressures to hear what is really troubling her. I have found many times that a nurse does not need to know the answer to every question or the exact analgesic or tranquilizer to give to her patients. Many times just taking the time to care about your patient as a person can eliminate the need for that medication we so quickly give to make them "comfortable," You need to be one of the nurses of the future who keeps the art of listening active and viable. Try it, they'll like it, and you will be amazed how many of your patients prefer you to be their nurse in the future.

Prayer

Sorry Lord, that I often don't even take the time to be silent before you in prayer. I'm so busy pitching my requests I just don't stop long enough to really hear you speak. Please help me, Holy Spirit, to turn off the world's distractions and hear what God is saying to me today. Help me to give this most precious commodity to my patients whenever I have a few moments not occupied by technical procedures. In the name of Jesus, the master of profound listening, I pray, Amen.

My Place in Time

I trust in you, O LORD; I say, "You are my God." My times are in your hands (Ps. 31:14-15).

It was spring break. One sunny afternoon, a friend and I visited a park in a neighboring town that was hosting a tribute to the Civil War. Old-fashioned buildings were strategically placed around a center lawn with dirt roads criss-crossing through. Locals were donned in traditional 1860s dress, giving the illusion we had entered through a door into the past. We hiked along one of the roads past merchants' shops to the battle field where some of the men were preparing to recreate the Battle of Culp's Hill. We chose a trail to the left and ended up on the confederate side overlooking a deep grassy valley with the Union troops on the hill beyond. The men and boys marched in companies: muskets, caps, and cannons with blanks within reach. Firing shattered the warmth and peace of the afternoon. It was frighteningly accurate as men would shoot, fall back to load, and shoot again. Each stared their opponent in the face all too aware of who they were aiming at. As I watched through the roar and smoke, some feigned death and injury. Nurses scurried behind the lines with water and bandages.

Generals on horses barked orders. It shocked me how real it all seemed. I was swept into the moment. "This is how it really was," I whispered to my friend. Men and boys really crossed a field similar to this one. It was really this noisy and smoky. At times people even stood like we are and watched. They watched oblivious to the blood, fear, and pain, attentive only to whether their side was winning. For a split second, I felt what it must have been like for someone to see their son or husband march down the hill, keeping their eyes fixed on the target, constantly praying they would stay standing when the smoke had cleared. How the nurses, must have dreaded going down to survey the damage, keenly aware of how little they could help. Real and surreal it must have been. As we made our way back down the hill toward the tiny town replica, we saw the wooden church perched on a small hill. God, you were there when the battle was real, when the clothes were newly styled, when the hitching posts weren't decoration, when people long gone were my age with a whole future ahead of them. You were there when I was only a "someday."[13]

Prayer

I am so thankful for this day of reminiscence. It has shown me how wonderful it is to work in nursing during this time of great technological advances, knowing that there are indeed many things I, as a nurse, can do to help my patients. It was wonderful to realize that you, God, are Lord yesterday, today and always, during all the changing seasons of life. How wonderful that you cared for each of those soldiers and nurses during the Civil War as well as each of us today. You have given each of us our place in time. All praise to you our redeemer and king! In Jesus' name, Amen.

Vindicated

May the LORD be our judge and decide between us. May he consider my cause and uphold it; may he vindicate me by delivering me from your hand (1 Sam. 24:15).

While I was staffing our unit one Wednesday, a student nurse with a searching judgment question approached me, she said, "Mrs. Azeem came back from surgery three hours ago and still has not requested anything for pain. When I asked her if she is uncomfortable she denied any pain. Should I just talk her into taking a hypo? I don't feel I have the right to insist when she knows her needs better than I do." She and I talked about the situation a few minutes more and then together decided that this student was doing the right thing by explaining the rationale for using pain medication postoperatively and then allowing Mrs. Azeem the power to decide. I felt the student was being very in tune with her patient and was showing Mrs. Azeem respect as an individual. This would give the patient a sense of control in an otherwise uncomfortably out-of-control circumstance.

An hour later, I overheard the nursing instructor berating this same student for not insisting that her patient take the hypo. She then made the student draw up the Demerol and Vistaril and give it to Mrs. Azeem. My heart sank. How demoralizing for the student! How infuriating for the patient! Every rule for patient empowerment had just been broken!

I conveyed the occurrence to my fellow nurses. Before the end of our shift, many of us had reassured the student of the inappropriateness of her instructor's actions. I also spoke with the instructor about patient empowerment and conveyed to her the good judgment skills this student had displayed before deciding to not give the medication against the patient's will.

I hoped that we had helped the student feel vindicated. I also hoped that this instructor would learn to be more sensitive to both her students and their patients. Then I personally thanked the Lord for allowing me to overhear this instructor-to-student conversation. I prayed that this experience would reinforce the student's confidence in her nursing judgment and that she would realize age and experience doesn't always correlate with wisdom. Some experienced people can be very naive and someone young in years can be very wise. Wisdom is a gift from the Lord and God's opinion is the only one we need to be concerned about. His approval is all we should seek.

Prayer

Be with each of us, Lord, as we make dozens of decisions every shift. Help us to always put our patients' concerns first. Help us to not be men-pleasers but seek to please only you for then we know that our decisions will always be correct. In Jesus' name, Amen.

Incompetence

Commit to the LORD whatever you do, and your plans will succeed (Prov. 16:3).

"Jack Lane is a seventy-eight year old man who has pneumonia. His main problem is he is so short of breath. His O2 is on 4L/NC. He gets S.O.B. even with talking. He's had his bath, but I had to do most of it for him. He wasn't able to walk today because he is so tired. The doctor has him on Zinacef IVPB for his antibiotic. He ate fifty percent of his breakfast and 30 percent of his lunch. He had a bowel movement today. His B.P. was high this morning, at 190/94, so I gave him some Procardia SL and it came down to 150/80. I guess that's all I have to report. Any questions?"

"When was Jack admitted? Does he have a history of other health problems? Who is the house officer following his care? Is his cough productive, and how do his lungs sound? What is his O2 Sat on four liters of O2? Does his doctor know that his blood pressure has been consistently getting higher? Is the MSW working on nursing home placement?"

Your first tension-filled inter-shift report is done. Your mind raced. You had hoped that you had covered most of what was important, but obviously what you reported was only the tip of the iceberg. You're thinking "I sure made a mess of the whole thing! Will I ever be able to keep it all organized? How will I ever learn to give the 3-11 p.m. nurse all the information she needs? I thought that I had given good care, but there are more things I should be doing in order to give comprehensive care."

Every R.N. has been where you are now to one degree or another. You will gradually think, learn, decipher, and move on to competency, but right now it looks overwhelming. Even after years of experience, there will be a day now and then when the workload or the high demands that nursing places on your mind, body, emotions, and organizational skills will cause you to come up short of what you feel you should have accomplished for your shift. "Sure," you say, "but I have so many of those days! I just get one area of my day together and another falls apart. Maybe I'm just not nurse material."

If the Lord wants you to be a nurse you will gradually "get your act together." Read our Proverbs passage for this week again, and take the pressure off yourself. Maybe God had a higher purpose in mind for your future as a mature Christian nurse than giving a perfect report would have thwarted. Rather than getting down on yourself because your pride was dented, delve introspectively into the day's events and glean what God is trying to teach you for the future date when you must give report. Start and end each work shift with a mind open to what God might want you to learn from each occurrence, and trust Him to give you wisdom. Then you will more and more often feel Him guiding your hands, pricking your memory, and putting words into your mouth. Also, always be humble enough to listen to shift reports given by veteran nurses, and learn their techniques. You will soon be giving a concise and comprehensive shift report after which very few questions will be asked. And remember that, no matter how well you do, there will always be certain people whom you can never satisfy. They may want you to do some of their work for them, and that's not your concern.

Prayer

Heavenly Father, please help me to get over my wounded pride and fear of failure; may the mistakes of this day be used by you to teach me to be a better nurse tomorrow. Thank you for making my mistakes ones that really didn't hurt my patient's recovery. And Holy Spirit, please guide me tomorrow toward greater success in the occupation I will dedicate daily to my Lord. In Jesus' name, Amen.

Full Disclosure

All men will hate you because of me... (Matt. 10:22).

Nursing has so many inspiring and heart-warming experiences, such as seeing a patient relax during a treatment because of your support, your explanation of what is to be expected, and your use of human touch to convey your empathy. Seeing a wound heal because of diligent treatment and timely antibiotics is so gratifying. Helping your patient attain total pain relief following orthopedic surgery because you have given the proper combination of anti-inflammatory medicines and analgesics, often gets you a resounding, "thank you."

In contrast, one situation you face will never become positive or common-place no matter how often you are exposed to it. The moment you accompany the surgeon as he tells a wife that her husband of forty years has inoperable pancreatic cancer with only three to six months to live, is one of those situations. The day your patient's daughter is told that her father's EEG shows no brain waves and she must decide whether or not to discontinue her father's ventilator support, is another one of these times. The horrendous revelation of ALS to a thirty year old mother of four young children brings feelings of injustice even if this is the tenth "bad news" scene you have participated in as a nurse. Most people appreciate hearing this straight talk about their prognosis, but the doctor cannot provide much comfort because there is no medical or surgical "silver bullet" to rectify any of these situations.

Jesus also practiced straight talk with his disciples. He told them that He would die at the hands of angry men. He, however, could add the solution that He would rise again on the third day. He warned them, in our verse for this week, that life as a follower of Christianity would be difficult, that ungodly people would hate them because of their beliefs, but He also assured them that they would have an eternal reward for diligence in their walk in the faith. He predicted His own return to heaven, leaving them without His daily presence. He did not leave them alone, impotent, or defenseless though as we sometimes feel when giving our patients news of terminal illness: He sent them the Holy Spirit to give companionship, power, and wise control of the circumstances they would face.

As modern day disciples of Jesus Christ, we have that same assurance, power, and peace. It will not change our circumstances when persecuted, but it will give us hope and endurance to claim all circumstances for God's glory.

Prayer

Dear Lord God Almighty, even though it hurts me to hear bad news given to my patients, I know that this is a part of being a nurse that will never cease. We live in a sinful, fallen world, and drastic illness and death are a perpetual part of it. Thank you for giving me the tools to conquer my world for your glory. Please help me to know when and how to use them in my work as a nurse and in my personal circumstances. In the Holy Spirit's power and Jesus' name I pray, Amen.

Sunset

Let them praise the name of the LORD, for his name alone is exalted; his splendor is above the earth and the heavens (Ps. 148:13).

"Use your eyes as if tomorrow you would be stricken blind. Greet the dawn eager to discover new beauties in nature."[14]

It's not the dawn you greet as you stare out your dorm-room window today. You'd probably had your head buried in your books for several hours when the change in the lighting of your room or the color dancing on the pages of your book suddenly changed, and you just felt the need to see what brought the change.

When you look out, your vision is literally assaulted by color—the most gorgeous sunset you have seen in weeks! Deep lavender clouds line the horizon. Hot pink sky dances between the black treetops. Above the treetops flows an unrestrainedly red radiance. All time should stop at this moment so you can have enough time to drink in all this beauty! For this minute, there is no homework to be done, no hunger, no worries about tomorrow, just peace and awe beyond your senses' abilities to take it all in. Freeze this time frame forever!

How majestic is our God, the God of creation! How artistic in His hues. How thoughtful of His created beings to give us such glorious colors to view and eyes to view them! Psalm 148 is a psalm of praise from all God's creation, a tribute to His power, His creativity, His faithfulness, and His love for us. What a privilege to be reminded, in the middle of our hectic pace of life of how awesome our God really is and to be reminded of the depth of His love for us. Instead of the tunnel vision we so often get trapped in, He wants all of us to keep the bigger brighter picture in focus and in the forefront.

Prayer

Dear Jesus, thank you for breaking into my thoughts and senses for just a few moments to quietly remind me of your awesome presence. *"Praise the LORD, O my soul; all my inmost being, praise his holy name. Praise the LORD, all his heavenly hosts, you his servants who do his will. Praise the LORD, all his works everywhere in his dominion* (Ps 103:21-22). Amen

A Fragrance for the Lord

Do not make any incense with this formula for yourselves; consider it holy to the LORD
(Exod. 30:37).

Psychologists say that the sense of smell is one of our mind's most powerful triggers for memory. This morning, that was definitely true for me. As
I stood in the cafeteria line, the smells of breakfast turned my thoughts to
Wednesday mornings at home, of eggs pan-fried and toast popped up. It
was always the quick breakfast of the week because it was Mom's day to leave the house
with us in order to attend her weekly Bible study.

How I wished I could go home to the security of that quick breakfast, the equal-
ly-as-quick words of encouragement of my family, and the last minute hug of my
mother as I left for school. How I needed that hug and those words, "I love you,
honey. I'll pray for your midterm, etc. Just do your best. That's all God or I ask."
Organic Chemistry's midterm, my speech in Public Communications class, and my
term paper for Psychology all had to be completed today! Well, it was too late to call
Mom now. She would have already left for church. I would just remember the

thoughts that this morning's fragrances had triggered and do my best.

Whenever we are faced with overwhelming circumstances, it is always our first inclination to try and escape to a safe and affirming place. When that is not possible, we must always remember that God will be with us at all times. He can empower us to success. Moses had work to do according to God's specifications in our Bible passage for this week. When his work was done, he was instructed to offer that work to the Lord. God promised to meet with him and to make all things anointed with this specific fragrance to be holy. As you go about your tasks today, remember that your Lord will meet with you. Offer your conquest of each personal challenge of your day to God as a fragrant offering. Then He will make you holy in all you do.

Prayer

I need your presence with me today, Lord. I cannot grasp the arms of my mother around me physically today, but I know she is thinking of me and that you are with me. I offer my best efforts to your glory and holiness. I pray that they will be a sweet fragrance to you. In Jesus, my Savior's name, I pray, Amen.

Silence is Golden

My dear brothers, take note of this: everyone should be quick to listen, slow to speak...
(Jas. 1:19).

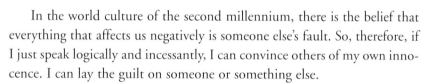

In the world culture of the second millennium, there is the belief that everything that affects us negatively is someone else's fault. So, therefore, if I just speak logically and incessantly, I can convince others of my own innocence. I can lay the guilt on someone or something else.

"Sure I was late getting to class but it wasn't my fault. There was a huge freight train at my crossing,, and it took up all of my extra time."

"Yes, I had a nasty argument with my roommate last night, but I couldn't avoid it because she's just so compulsive. I could never keep her satisfied with how I clean the apartment, so I just don't try anymore."

"Of course I spoke up against Molly at the Nurses' Station today. She's just such an airhead. I had to correct her right then and there before she gave us all a bad reputation with the supervising R.N.s."

"Well, yes, I got a 'D' on my last biochemistry test. I couldn't help it. My high school friends came to visit. You wouldn't expect me to be so impolite as to not entertain them after they came all that way, would you? Can I take a re-test?"

These are just a few examples of how we all try to elevate our own status at the expense of others, how we talk and talk all around a circumstance until we feel free of the burden of our own behavior. Very seldom do we hear anyone give an uninvolved "yes" or "no" and leave it at that. Jesus Christ, our mentor, exemplifies the art of direct speech. He makes no excuses, He blames no one else for His predicament, and His words of response are few.

How are you doing with learning to control your tongue? Are you able to hit a negative circumstance head on, keep your answer brief, and refrain from placing the blame on someone else? If you can, you're a better person than most. Society's attitudes can so easily seep into our own behavior that, before we know it, we're following their example of shifting blame by incessant talking to justify our actions.

Try to focus on Christ's example this week and into the following months. Be honest in all your conversations. Own up to any mistake you make and refrain from placing blame. When accused rightly or wrongly, it is not necessary for you to counter attack. Remember, as Sam Rayburn once said, "The unspoken word never defeats one. What one does not say does not have to be explained."[15] Silence can be very valuable, as valuable as gold.

Prayer

Dear Jesus, what a fine example you have given us of standing on the truth and defending it without saying hardly anything. I need your help this week to refrain from being defensive and accusatory or a second millennial escapist. In your strength, I press on, Amen.

God's Waiting Room

I waited patiently for the LORD; he turned to me and heard my cry (Ps. 40:1).

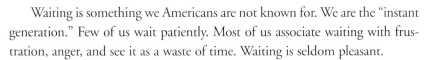

Waiting is something we Americans are not known for. We are the "instant generation." Few of us wait patiently. Most of us associate waiting with frustration, anger, and see it as a waste of time. Waiting is seldom pleasant.

Hospitals are one giant waiting room. We wait in the admitting registration area, then we wait for our lab work to be drawn, and then we wait twice as long in the radiology department.

We nurses often send visitors to our units to waiting rooms while we perform procedures on their relative or friend. In the hospital, about the only time we think of waiting as an enjoyable experience is when a father is waiting to hear of the birth of his baby.

In the Bible passage that you are asked to read and meditate on for this week, we see Samuel's mother, Hannah, in her own personal waiting room. Her waiting period was very long, very frustrating, and very painful. Because of the mores of her day, she was humiliated monthly. Added to her pain of not being able to conceive were the taunts of her husband's diabolical second wife! How did she react? Not with outward anger or revengeful behavior. She continued to worship God and trust Him for an answer even when God's ears seemed deaf to her anguished cries. She waited for years. She persevered in hope of a future answer. What a wonderful example of how to wait on the Lord! Then, when God did remove her from His waiting room by answering her prayers for a son, she dedicated that son to the Lord. She gave back to God the gift He had finally given to her.

How are you doing in God's waiting room? (We all have been there many times, you know.) Are you lashing out at your tormentors or those who already have what you are waiting for? Are you quietly weeping before God? Are you angry with God for making you wait? Are you continuing to worship Him even though He seems deaf to your prayers? Have you stopped praying because God just answers "no" all the time? I hope that you have or will follow Hannah's example by trusting that God is listening, that He loves you and cares about your life, that He has the power to change what you want changed, and that you can rest in His wisdom and plan for your circumstances even if His answer is "no."

Prayer

Oh Lord Almighty, I beseech you to look upon this servant's misery and remember me as you remembered Hannah. Give me the peace of mind to know that you always listen to me. Give me patience in your waiting room, Lord. As I persevere in communication with you, as I trust in your wisdom to know what is best for me, help me to see your hand drawing me out of the waiting room and onto the path you want me to walk. In Jesus' name I pray, Amen.

Cheating

Oh great and powerful God, whose name is the LORD Almighty, great are your purposes and mighty are your deeds. Your eyes are open to the ways of men; you reward everyone according to his conduct and as his deeds deserve (Jer. 32:18-19).

In this passage of Genesis, we see Abraham and Sarah being visited by angels of the Lord. There are even some who believe that one of the visitors at Mamre was the Lord Jesus Himself. They came with unbelievably wonderful news for this couple. The Lord would bless them in their old age with a son!

Abraham and Sarah had been childless for many years, and Sarah was past her child-bearing years. It is, therefore, easy to understand her doubts about the validity of the angels' message. Sarah's greatest mistake was not that she doubted the Lord's promise, but that she lied about her doubt because she was afraid of the consequences.

This story and the verses in Jeremiah speak to us also. Over the years of schooling, and even now in nursing school, there are classmates who, out of fear of failing or fear of getting an unacceptable grade which is lower than they need to retain their scholarship, will cheat on tests or quizzes. Many times, they get a better grade than others who study just as hard but resist the temptation to cheat. And to top the list of aggravations, they will often lie to the professor when confronted about it. Sometimes the professor cannot prove his accusation, and they "get away" with their dishonesty.

When you are tempted to also cheat because the results seem so profitable, remember Jeremiah 32:18-19. The Lord knows about your honesty, and He sees their lies. He will reward you in the future for your virtue. Right now, you have done what is right in God's eyes. Your classmate may seem to be getting the better end of the deal at this point in time, but God sees their ways. He will "reward" them for their deeds also. Yield not to temptation!

Prayer

Help me, Lord, to hold fast to the principles that I know you command in the Bible. The temptations in my world can be so strong because I don't always see the punishment you mete out to those who disobey. Please help me not to judge others or compare my behavior to their actions because I have my own areas of imperfection. Jesus, who resisted all temptations, is my strength, for in his name I pray, Amen.

Transferring God's Touch

She said to herself, "If I only touch his cloak, I will be healed (Matt. 9:21).

"Betsy, if you are caught up with your patient care plans and charting, you might want to watch the central line insertion in Room 503. They will be starting in a few minutes."

"Thank you, Ms. Timmerman. I'm all caught up and I would love to watch."

Because you are as anxious to learn new procedures as any student nurse, you find your spot as an observer in Room 503 along with two other students. In addition to noting the equipment needed for the procedure and the steps taken in the procedure itself, you notice what the R.N. assisting the physician does with regard to the patient. She explains, in minute detail, exactly the order of events and how the patient will feel during each step. She establishes eye contact with her patient, voice contact, emotional contact, and holds her hand. She attempts to ascertain any discomfort or fears her patient may be having while she hands the doctor the betadine, lidocaine, I.V. tubing, etc. that he needs to complete his task. She communicates any patient concerns to the doctor if they are something under his control to correct. Finally, she comfortingly holds the patient's hand when the discomfort must simply be borne. It's the nurse's touch and verbal distraction that can determine the patient's long-term memory of this procedure as a tolerable or intolerable one.

This week's scripture in Matthew tells of several people who knew the value of touch. Of course, Jesus' touch was much more powerful than our touch as nurses can be. He was able to heal without anyone's assistance and no modern medical procedures. As our example, He shows us, however, how commonplace emotional connections and physical contact are ways of showing Christ's love. This subclavian insertion, along with many other nurse-physician actions, could be accomplished as well mechanically by any nurse, but it is the empathy of this nurse that flavors her patient's view of her hospital stay. May God bless you each day as you distribute your touch of the Master's hand to each of your patients.

Prayer

Jesus, I am so thankful for your powerful examples in the Bible of the value of touch in our interactions with other people. Thank you also for arranging this observation to include a compassionate doctor and nurse who modeled for me the godly approach to patient care. Help me, Lord, to be a model of your love to my patients as these two professionals have been for me. In the strength of your Spirit I pray, Amen.

How Are You?

I know what it is to be in need, and I know what it is to have plenty. I have learned the secret of being content in any and every situation (Phil. 4:12).

Probably the most common question asked in the English language is, "How are you?" It's asked so often that we many times answer, "Fine. How are you?" when we really don't feel so well or we really are emotionally upset at the time. We quite frequently don't give an honest answer to this overused question.

Life is almost always a mountaintop or valley experience. Few days find any of us on the plains. Hopefully you and I have many days of exuberant joy and mellow happiness, but our days can also be inundated with trying circumstances, frustrations, and ill health. Many days we wish we could change things. If we choose to dwell on the down in the valley moments, we could easily become bogged down.

A more honest answer to this question might be, "Fine, under the circumstances." Paul is our excellent example of how we as Christians do not necessarily need to become overpowered by happenings in our lives. Paul had been in prison. He had been gnawingly hungry. He had been put on a pedestal. He had been well taken care of. He had been highly praised, but he had also had attempts made to take his life. In all of these circumstances, however, Paul's reaction to life was always the same: contentment.

Today, as you experience the full range of situations or just peacefully coast through the minutes, remember Paul's example. You do not need to feel "under the circumstances." You can always feel "on top of things." Such a contented attitude comes from realizing that all that happens today is in God's plan for your life, and He will not only be by your side to help you through the hard times, but He will also program several good times into the minutes ahead. How are you, under the circumstances or on top of things?

Prayer

Thank you, Lord Jesus, for giving me a multitude of enlightening, elating, and edifying experiences in my life! Help me to count every moment of them by slowing the forward motion of my day to recognize how often these wonderful things happen. I want to focus also on the progress I am making toward being the best person and nurse I am capable of becoming. Do not let me become weighed down by things out of my control, and enable me to put all of life's occurrences into a wise perspective. Help me to labor with diligence and hope while you work out today's finished product. In love, optimism, and faith, I rely on your Holy Spirit's leading, Amen.

A Banana Split Sunday

Remember the Sabbath day by keeping it holy....For in six days the LORD made the heavens and the earth... but he rested on the seventh day (Exod. 20:8-11).

Sunday morning, depending on how you look at it, is the end of a busy week or the beginning of a new one. As a Christian, you know it is commanded by God to be a day for you to rest. God even showed us the necessity of a day of rest by His own example. This is when you begin to feel like you're being split apart. You are excited about going home to see your family and looking forward to returning to your home church for a service. In opposition to these feelings is the realization that you have so much homework this weekend, even if you skipped church you wouldn't have enough time to finish it all. Then too, there is the awful feeling of having to leave home and face the rat race at school again on Monday. Once you are home, you realize how much you have missed your parents and siblings. Then it's hard to go back to your dorm room. On top of this is the temptation to skip church with the logical excuse that you just can't spare the time. Also, maybe staying at college would be easier on your emotions because going home just makes you feel lost between two worlds.

The pain of the repeated breakaway makes you wonder if you should avoid the whole scene and just stay on campus to study. This makes you the banana split on Sunday.

The Lord knows how busy you are, but He still commands you to rest on the seventh day. God is our own best example. The work of creation certainly could have continued through Sunday, but he rested instead. God knows the innate human need our bodies have for rest. If we ignore this need, either physical or emotional sickness often forces us to rest when we least expect it or can least afford it.

God also knows the pain you feel at leaving home again on Sunday night. After all, He sent His Son out of His presence for thirty years! Jesus knows the temptation we face to just keep studying and forget about spiritual and physical fortification. In His confrontation with the devil in the wilderness, on the mountaintop, and on the pinnacle of the temple (Matt. 4:1-11), He demonstrated how we can resist the sinful urgings to put God and worship on the back burner.

So, pack that overnight bag, grab your car keys, and head home. Home to your family who is missing you and home to God's house to commune with your God who knows so well what you are dealing with. Then begin another week with rest and renewed energy, the spiritual and emotional uplift only God can give you through time spent in His presence.

Prayer

Lord, my Father, I am so grateful for the birth of your son into human form. I know He understands in a personal way the decisions and temptations I face. Thank you also for your poignant example of our human need for rest and worship. Thank you for a family who loves me so much it's hard to say "good-bye" again. Please help me to finish my homework even though I have less actual time to do it because I took the time to keep in touch with my earthly family and with you. In your son, Jesus' name I pray, Amen.

Don't Lose It

Everyone should be quick to listen, slow to speak, and slow to become angry (Jas.1:19).

"Your temper is one of your most valuable possessions. Don't lose it."[16] What a curious and clever way to look at anger. Have you ever really thought of anger as valuable? It is most often thought of as a vice. The Bible agrees with the statement above, however. Many times, the Scriptures remind us of how slow to anger and abounding in love our God is. With the supreme ruler of the universe as our example, we too need to learn to be in control of our frustrations and their resultant outbursts of anger.

When your instructor hands you an involved assignment for the weekend right after you just took his monstrous test and handed in your research paper on Friday, it would be very easy to lose your composure with him. When your patient refuses to follow any of your teaching instructions because she chooses to ignore her new diagnosis of diabetes and wants you to leave her alone, you can rightfully feel impatience, frustration, and anger with her. When your roommate leaves the sink full of dirty dishes for the third day in a row and you have no clean glass to drink your pop out of because she hasn't kept up her end of the apartment agreements, you can feel very justified in becoming angry with her.

Before you let any words come out of your mouth, remember what God's Word says about anger. He doesn't forbid all anger, but He wants us to persevere in our exercise of self-control so that our anger is always measured and righteous when vented. Before saying anything, consider the dissension your verbalization of angry feelings will cause in your relationship with your instructor. Try to look at the assignment the way he does and see the valuable lesson he is trying to teach you by giving it. Give him the benefit of the doubt as God has given to you when you do things of which He doesn't approve. Will analyzing the situation help you to see that your instructor is just doing his job well and preparing you thoroughly for your occupation? Putting yourself in your patient's place may help you understand how intimidating her new diagnosis must be for her. That, in turn, will probably help to diffuse your anger and give you the forbearance to give her repetitive instructions in the future when she is more emotionally able to handle the reality of her illness. You probably have a right to scream at your roommate because today's sink full of dirty dishes is not her first delinquency. Before you do so, however, remind yourself of how slow to anger God has been with you. He is totally perfect. Can you imagine His frustration every time you repeat that pet sin? Yet, He is self-controlled and loving enough to forgive you again and again and again. Therefore, in your striving to live the righteous life that God desires of you as His child, consider your anger as a valuable asset you just can't afford to lose.

Prayer

Dear Father, you are the example I daily try to follow. You are so patient and loving with me even though I repeat the same sins over and over. Please help me also to control my temper and it's verbalization. Give me more love for my fellowman so that I will take the time to walk in his shoes and attempt to understand his viewpoint more thoroughly before I explode at him. I appreciate all the help you will give me in learning more patience, in holding back my temper, and even dispelling the anger altogether. In Jesus' name I make these requests and await your Spirit's power to assist me, Amen.

"Smiley"

A happy heart makes the face cheerful (Prov. 15:13).

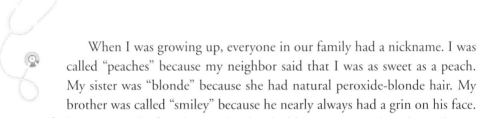

When I was growing up, everyone in our family had a nickname. I was called "peaches" because my neighbor said that I was as sweet as a peach. My sister was "blonde" because she had natural peroxide-blonde hair. My brother was called "smiley" because he nearly always had a grin on his face. I can testify, however, to the fact that my brother had his moments when the smile was gone. For instance, I don't recall seeing that smile when he was bickering with me at the breakfast table almost every morning. Nor do I think he would describe me as sweet as a peach when he invaded my territory while my teenage friends were over to visit. But to the general "public" our nicknames were appropriate ninety percent of the time.

"A smile is something that costs nothing but gives much. It enriches those who receive it, without making those who give it poorer. It takes but a moment but the memory of it sometimes lasts forever. None is so rich or mighty that they can get along without it, and none is so poor but that they can be made rich by it. A smile creates happiness in a home and fosters friendship in social settings. It brings rest to the weary, cheer to the discouraged, sunshine to the sad, and it is nature's best antidote for trouble. Yet it cannot be bought, begged, borrowed, or stolen for it is something that is of no value to anyone until it is given away. Some people are too tired to give you a smile. Give them one of yours, as none needs a smile so much as the one who has no more energy to give one."[17]

If someone were to give you a nickname today, what would it be? Would it be complimentary? Could your nickname also be "smiley"? One day at a time, try giving those around you the gift that costs nothing but may be so valuable to the person to whom you give it. It could change the entire outlook of that person's day. It could re-establish her belief in the goodness of life. It could make him realize the world would be lacking something valuable if he were not a productive part of it. As a Christian, whether financially poor or rich, whether carefree or burdened with pressures or sorrows, we still have so much to be joyful about! We have the love of the almighty God of heaven and earth! We have the comfort of His presence with us, the promise of forgiveness of our sins, and the hope of eternal life after physical death. So, from a happy heart, give the world a cheerful face. Smile!

Prayer

Thank you, Jesus, for your gracious and awesome gift of salvation! Because of your gift, I can have a happy heart and a joyful outlook on life even in unjust, cruel, pressurized, or sorrowful situations. The hope you have given me is indescribable. I adore you, Lord, Amen.

Care Plans

The LORD foils the plans of the nations....But the plans of the LORD stand firm forever, the purposes of his heart through all generations (Ps. 33:10).

The words of this week's title bring definite mental pictures to every present and former student nurse's mind. The picture is seldom a positive one. The amount of time involved in preparing care plans is their major drawback. The demand of vigilant concentration on picayune details, and the oppressive hawking of every nursing instructor attempting to find something missing in your analysis, all make care plans every student nurse's nightmare. Add to this the frustration of knowing that nursing school is the only time you will ever have to actually be this thorough when writing them. From the time of graduation onward, computer care plans will be the norm. Therefore, the hours spent in their composition will always feel futile.

Contrast this to the care plan God has for us all. Every detail of His plan is vitally important and has a definite purpose. (Of course, your nursing care plans also have a defining purpose; making you aware of every need your patient has in order to heal.)

God's plan involves no work on our part, just an acceptance of His free gift of salvation. God is not looking over our shoulder trying to find our mistakes in life. He is offering forgiveness of all the mistakes we make. His care plan was in effect before we were born; it will direct our steps throughout our entire lifespan on earth and culminate in an eternity within His presence. His plan is for all time and never needs updating. What is this care plan of God for us? The Lord declared, *"I will make a new covenant with the house of Israel* (Heb. 8:8). *"I will put my laws in their minds and write them on their hearts. I will be their God and they will be my people"* (Heb. 8:10). *"They will all know me from the least to the greatest"* (Heb 8:11). *"I will forgive their wickedness and will remember their sins no more"* (Heb. 8:12). *"Christ is the mediator of the new covenant, that those who are called may receive the promised eternal inheritance—now that he has died as a ransom to set them free from the sins committed"* (Heb. 9:15).

Have you grabbed hold of God's care plan for you? If not, I pray that you will accept God's free gift of salvation soon and beg to be in sync with His plans for your life on earth and for eternity.

Prayer

Your plan for me is truly a "care" plan, Lord. It is tailored to my personality and pertinent for all situations I will encounter. Thank you, Jesus, for giving the ultimate sacrifice to fulfill the Father's care plan for me. In deep gratitude and in Jesus' name. Amen.

Giving to the Lord

"Bring the whole tithe into the storehouse....Test me in this," says the LORD *Almighty, "and see if I will not open the floodgates of heaven and pour out so much blessing that you will not have room enough for it"* (Mal. 3:10).

What a great feeling to have your paycheck in your hand. You've worked a lot of hard hours between classes to accumulate this money. Now comes the difficult part of deciding what bills need paying the soonest. Let's see, there is gas for your car, groceries to re-supply, and a desperately needed haircut. When everything is subtracted from the total, you sure hope there is some money left over to buy that pair of slacks you saw at Sears. You start planning when you can go to the mall and whom you can go with. Your spirits soar. What fun it will be to shop for something other than the necessities for once! Then a little voice inside your head says, "What about your church tithe?" Your spirits plunge. There go your slacks and your day of shopping! Maybe I could just wait and pay my tithe out of my next paycheck. Would the Lord really care? After all He owns the world. He doesn't really "need" my money. He knows I'm "good for it." Then your conscience gets into the act, and you know in your heart that you need to tithe and forget about buying your slacks. You

149

grudgingly release your entire mall visiting dreams from your thoughts. Your tithe will be given, but not very cheerfully.

God says to you, in our verse for the week, "Give me your whole tithe and in return I will bless you beyond belief," Will this blessing be in the form of money? Probably nothing that tangible, but God will bless you for your obedience. Now if only you could also change your attitude, giving to the Lord generously and cheerfully. In 2 Corinthians 9:6-8, the apostle Paul, inspired by the Holy Spirit, tells us that if you sow sparingly, you will reap sparingly. If you give generously, you will receive generously from the Lord. Then Paul says, *"God will make all grace abound to you so that in all things and at all times you will have all you need and you will abound in all good works."* Obedience is commanded, but attitude changes the one blessed and the blessing.

Prayer

Dear Father in heaven, you are so generous with me! You give me a blessing just for having the right attitude and being obedient to your commands. Please help me to realize that I don't really "need" more clothes. That I can still have the fun of going to the mall with my friend and just buy something that does fit into my budget. Assist me in an attitude change so I can give to you cheerfully and generously every paycheck. I await your blessings from your storehouse. Love you. In Jesus' name, Amen.

People Watching

How many are your works, O LORD! In wisdom you made them all; the earth is full of your creatures (Ps. 104:24).

Are you a people watcher? I am. I find I thoroughly enjoy sitting in a park or standing in the foyer of a public auditorium observing individuals as they walk past. Some of them are dressed to the hilt. Some of them are dressed down to almost too-casual attire. Some are sauntering. Some are rushing to meet an unknown deadline. Some are animated in conversation. Some are totally quiet and introspective. Smiles adorn many faces, but once in a while you see a face engulfed in total sadness.

The variety of God's created beings just in the human category is endless. There are so many different mannerisms, so many personalities, different mouths, eyes, ears, and noses in a hundred different shapes, sizes, and colorings. There is hair of differing lengths, styles and hues, and lack of hair in varying degrees of regress on each person's head.

If you have a moment some day and it doesn't sound too boring to you, take the time to sit in your hospital's main entrance or a waiting room and watch each person as he comes through the door. Exercise your nursing observation skills and emotional keenness trying to decipher why this person is smiling or why another is sad. Try to ascertain why each person has dressed the way he does. Is his or her clothing showing a lifestyle or an attitude or a certain personality trait? You will see people you wish to emulate, others you feel sorry for, and some that are just totally fascinating because of their escape from any norm. Right about now, you might be thinking, "Why would I want to waste my valuable time in such a worthless activity?" I suggest this to you because this activity is actually very educational. These moments will increase the accuracy of your assessment skills as a nurse. Emotionally, you will find yourself more open to the inner workings of your patients' minds. You will also be amazed at the creative genius of our God. How could He have possibly thought of all the combinations that exist both physically and psychologically in conglomerate humanity? What a great artist our God is!

As you observe this entourage of men and women, children and babies, you will see how each of them interacts with each other and their environment. Many people are nondescript with regard to displaying any unusual action or visage. Some are shy or quiet. Other people are gregarious or talkative. Each one, however, gives out a unique aura and persona. Each person has people who love and appreciate him. Each individual has a specific role to play in your community. God created each person's "style" in a very deliberate way. Each human being is special to his creator.

Prayer

Lord God, your creative power is truly awesome and unfathomable! How inept I feel in comparison. That very ineptness makes me realize how much I need your power in my relationships with my family, friends, coworkers, and patients. It also makes me realize there is no one right appearance or personality. Every one of us is equally important to you. Thank you for that knowledge. It helps me to feel valuable as a person and makes me aware of the value of each person I encounter. In Jesus' name, He who accepted everyone equally, I pray, Amen.

A Vow Made—A Vow Paid

It is a trap for a man to dedicate something rashly and only later to consider his vows
(Prov. 20:25).

It's exam time. The crunch is on. Whether you have studied hard or hardly studied, this will be the time of reckoning.

What a paradox examination time brings. It's usually a beautiful time of the year with the warm weather of spring outside, so it's hard to concentrate on the task at hand. You're excited about being done for the summer break, but before you can enjoy it, you need to get some acceptable grades on your exams in order to pass to the next level of nursing school. The panic sets in when you see how much material the exam covers, yet you are tempted to just bag it and rely on what's already stored in your gray matter.

Exam time is often a time of vow making. "Lord, if you'll only get me a 'B' on this microbiology exam, I'll promise to study harder next year." "If you help me to decipher just the right fundamentals in nursing to cram into my head, I'll do anything you want me to do." Does this sound familiar?

If you have made promises like these to God in moments of desperation, you're not the only one. It's easy to make vows in the heat of crises. Keeping the vow is another matter. Our passage for this week shows us that keeping a promise is a definite act of the will. And that keeping your vow has a twofold positive effect:

1. You will have a clear conscience before God.
2. You will maintain a correct relationship with God that makes it easier to ask another favor of Him in the future.

So as you make your vows this week, be sure to keep them specific and attainable. Then, once God has answered your request, be sure to fulfill your vow quickly and completely.

Prayer

Precious Savior, you are our exquisite example of how to keep a vow. You kept your vow all the way to the cross. As I study diligently, I ask that you will bless my efforts with success, and I will strive in return to keep any promises I have made. Amen.

One Rung Attained

Only let us live up to what we have already attained (Phil. 3:16).

Hallelujah! Praise the Lord! It's done. The first year of nursing school is completed. All that pressing on, taking hold, and straining toward the goal has paid off. Your grades were adequate enough to encourage you to move ahead another level after a vacation break. What exhilaration you feel! What a sense of accomplishment! What relief to have made it this far!

As you pack up your belongings once more to head home, there is probably a small feeling of reminiscence. Remember how intimidated you felt that first day as you shuffled these same boxes of clothes you are now re-packing? Remember how badly your hands trembled when you gave your first shot? Remember how often you wondered if you had the will and maturity to stick it out until the end of the year? Yet here you are, a seasoned college student and a nurse well on her/his way to becoming a professional.

You have learned so much! You have grown in decision-making ability. You have honed your interpersonal relationship skills. Your brain has expanded exponentially in its knowledge of medicine and nursing practice. You have progressed in bringing everything under God's control rather than your own control.

As you look forward to some well-earned relaxation time and renewed times with your family, you needn't have any regrets. Enjoy your time off. Just live up to what you have already attained.

It is my hope that you have grown in your knowledge of the Bible this year. Hopefully you have become more attuned to God's leading in your everyday circumstances. I implore you to take no vacation from the Lord during this time of freedom from classroom schedules. Make Jesus a partner in all your playtimes, and keep pressing on toward the goal of becoming more Christ-like in all you do. *Shalom!*

Prayer

"I exalt you my God the King; I will praise your name forever and ever. Great is the LORD *and most worthy of praise; his greatness no one can fathom"* (Ps. 154:1,3). *"You open your hand and satisfy the desires of every living thing. The* LORD *watches over all who love him.… My mouth will speak in praise of the* LORD*"* (Ps. 145:16,20-21). In Jesus' name, Amen and Amen.

Endnotes

---

[1] Julian Jaynes, "Thrust into the Sky," *Illustrations Unlimited*, ed. by James Hewitt (Wheaton: Tyndale House Publishers,Inc., 1988), p 414.

[2] Phillips Brooks, "Becoming Spiritual," *Illustrations Unlimited*, p. 188.

[3] Written by Tami Seif-Pothoven, daughter of the author and fellow R.N.

[4] Written by Tami Seif-Pothoven.

[5] "Cautious Investment," *Illustrations Unlimited*, p. 204.

[6] Written by Tami Seif-Pothoven.

[7] "Jesus Is All the World to Me," *New Christian Hymnal*, ed. by Rev. H.J. Kuiper, (Grand Rapids: Wm. B. Eerdmans Publishing Co., 1929), p. 398.

[8] "Don't Quit," author unknown.

[9] "They Will Know We Are Christians by our Love," *Hymns For the Family of God,* (Nashville: Paragon Associates, Inc.,1976), p. 677.

[10] Written by Tami Seif-Pothoven.

[11] Samuel Butler, "The Secret of Progress," *Illustrations Unlimited,* p. 343.

[12] Henri Nouwen, "The Need for Balance," *Illustrations Unlimited*, p. 318.

[13] Written by Tami Seif-Pothoven.

[14] Helen Keller, "Seeking the Light," *Illustrations Unlimited*, p. 259.

[15] Sam Rayburn, "Silence is Golden," *Illustrations Unlimited*, p. 474.

[16] "Hold on Tight," *Illustrations Unlimited*, p. 33.

[17] "A Smile," *Illustrations Unlimited*, p. 278.